Understanding England's Cathedrals

Dave Hennis was born in 1952 and raised in a cathedral city (Peterborough); he obtained a BA degree in Architecture in another (London, which contains 15% of the country's cathedrals) and has lived in a third (St Albans). He spent all his working life in the construction industry before retiring in 2013. Dave has travelled extensively around England, Europe and the rest of the World with his wife Sue. These experiences have provided the inspiration, the ideas, the knowledge and the time to research and write this, his first book. The aim of this book is to increase readers' knowledge of England's cathedrals that should help make future visits to these endearingly popular buildings more comprehensible and enjoyable. It will look at how a cathedral's history, location, patron, financing, purpose, design and building have shaped its appearance, size and layout.

Understanding England's Cathedrals

Dave Hennis

Arena Books

First published in 2015 by Arena Books
Arena Books
6 Southgate Green
Bury St. Edmunds
IP33 2BL

www.arenabooks.co.uk
Distributed in America by Ingram International, One Ingram Blvd., PO Box
3006, La Vergne, TN 37086-1985, USA.

Dave Hennis
   Understanding England's Cathedrals

British Library cataloguing in Publication Data. A catalogue record for this Book is
available from the British Library.

ISBN-13   978-1-909421-61-5

BIC classifications:- ANX, AMN, AMA, AMC, AMG.

Printed and bound by Lightning Source UK

Cover design
by Jason Anscomb

Typeset in
Times New Roman

CONTENTS

List of photographs, illustrations, maps, diagrams, tables and acknowledgements.

....

Acknowledgements

To Alan Stewart, a life-long Christian, for all his help and advice.

To Ruth Stewart for proof-reading and commenting on the text.

To Dave Beech for his maps of Anglo-Saxon and present-day England.

To Michael Blandford for his photographs and advice on the statues at Wells Cathedral.

To Pamela Stirling LRPS for her photographs and advice on Exeter Cathedral's misericords.

To all the Cathedral Guides I have met for their time, enthusiasm and knowledge.

To the many Friends of English cathedrals who submitted photographs which I have acknowledged above.

And last but not least, to my wife Sue for putting up with my frequent absences during this book's 18 month gestation period and for proof-reading all the drafts.

1. INTRODUCTION
What is the purpose of this book?

A re you one of the 15 million people who visited an English cathedral this year and were overwhelmed by its size, grandeur and architecture, baffled by its symbolism, layout and artwork and wondered.......................? Why was it built here and what was so special about this place? Who was the patron and organisation that commissioned its building? Who paid for it and where did they get their money from? How much did it cost? Why is it so big? What functions did it perform? Why is it shaped like it is? Who designed it? Where did the ideas come from? How was it erected before reinforced concrete, juggernauts and tower cranes were invented? Who built it? How has it changed since it was first built? What were the old buildings adjoining it used for? How does it differ from European cathedrals? Is it still used today?

If you have asked similar questions and are seeking the answers, then this book is for you. Its aim is to complement, not replace, the excellent guided tours and monographs available on individual cathedrals and to give the native visitor and the overseas tourist a better overall knowledge of English history, religion, architecture and building technology in one easily-read volume. Your increased understanding will hopefully make future visits to some of England's finest and most popular buildings even more comprehensible, enjoyable and rewarding.

The ancient cathedral was seen as the pinnacle of medieval society's spiritual, cultural and technical competence, employing the best designers, artists, craftsmen and materials that the available money could buy. They developed, along with the monasteries, into enlightened enclaves of worship, learning, hospitality, art, music, agriculture and medicine in an often chaotic, violent outside world. A change of religion, rulers and constitution, wars, competition between patrons, new money-making ideas, innovative architectural styles, dubious reconstructions, fires and building failures has meant that they have been constantly rebuilt and altered throughout their 1,700 years of history.

England's cathedrals were and are full of superlatives. Lincoln Cathedral's 175 metre spire was the world's tallest structure from 1311 until it collapsed in 1549, never to be rebuilt; Salisbury's surviving 123 metre high spire, was the tallest edifice in England until as recently as 1964; London's Old St Paul's, burnt down in 1666, was at one-eighth of a mile in length the longest church ever erected while Liverpool's Anglican Cathedral, only completed in 1978, is currently the seventh largest church in the world.

Yet the English cathedral we see today is a mere skeleton of what it once was. Their vivid wall paintings, medieval coloured glass, ornate shrines and statues have all disappeared. Whole elements, chapels, cloisters and monastic communal buildings, have been demolished while parts have variously been used as shops, theatres, meeting halls, courts, workshops, short-cuts, prisons and even for stabling horses. Despite all this, the centuries of iconoclasm and zeal of Victorian restorers, English cathedrals have somehow managed to retain some of Europe's finest range of original, reasonably complete, fixtures and fittings.

Today visitors to England's cathedrals vastly outnumber worshippers, the consequence of the increased popularity in the tourist and heritage industries. London's St Paul's Cathedral and Westminster Abbey are both in this country's top ten of its most visited buildings, each attracting over two million visitors annually. Canterbury Cathedral has one million tourists every year, roughly equivalent to half of England's entire population when the Norman's rebuilt it in the late 11th Century. Their current popularity and indeed their very survival has not always been so assured. A 17th Century debate in the Houses of Parliament proposed to demolish all of England's cathedrals and give the money raised to feed the poor. A couple of centuries later two of England's most famous cathedrals came close to being torn down because they were thought to be too badly decayed to be economically restored.

Viewed from a modern day perspective, their history includes the bizarre and the tragic. In 1538 a representative of the king appeared in front of a cathedral shrine and ordered the interned to attend a meeting to answer a charge of treason. His subsequent non-appearance was deemed to prove his guilt and so he posthumously lost his sainthood, his remains were exhumed and burnt while his shrine was dismantled. Over 1,500 Scottish prisoners-of-war died after being incarcerated in a cathedral during the English Civil Wars while a future cathedral was demolished overnight in 1723 by a gang of labourers employed by a solitary cleric because of its parlous state.

Visitors from Europe will notice some fundamental differences between English medieval cathedrals and their Continental counterparts. In this country, cathedrals tend to stand apart from the adjoining city within a quiet precinct enclosed by high walls. They are generally considerably longer and are not as tall: Beauvais Cathedral in France is some 17 metres taller than this country's highest whilst no overseas cathedral can compete with Winchester's overall length of 181.75 metres. Surviving spires are rare (Salisbury, Norwich and

Lichfield are the exception), west fronts less elaborate (Wells, Exeter and Peterborough apart) and have more austere interiors possessing none of the highly decorated wall paintings and floor coverings found typically in a European Catholic cathedral.

For the purposes of brevity, this book will adhere strictly to the definition of a cathedral, namely a church that contains the bishop's 'cathedra' (Latin for seat) from where he or she oversees their area of responsibility known as a diocese or see. These churches were built to a grander size and splendour than others in this area. Today they offer daily, high quality services and music, performing an important role in the civic and communal life of both their city and the surrounding region particularly at major festival times and to commemorate notable events, appointments and deaths. Over one hundred churches possessing these characteristics were built in the Middle Ages with just over a quarter having been used as a cathedral at one time or another. So Westminster and Glastonbury Abbeys will form part of this book's narrative as they were cathedrals for just 33 years whilst equally impressive Tewkesbury and Beverley Minsters are excluded as they have never housed a bishop's seat. For the same reason some very modest and architecturally insignificant Anglo-Saxon cathedrals are included, whilst other far more noteworthy contemporary churches have been ignored.

The Anglican Church of England is the state religion possessing 42 cathedrals served by 40 diocesan bishops. Recent changes mean that Bradford, Ripon and Wakefield have cathedrals but no diocesan bishop whilst the city of Leeds, England's third largest, currently has the latter but not the former. Today these three Yorkshire cities, along with 67 other towns and areas, are served by a suffragan or assistant bishop who comes under the authority of a diocesan bishop. Overseeing the bishops are two archbishops: the Archbishop of Canterbury (known as the Primate of All England) and his deputy, the Archbishop of York (Primate of England) who is responsible for the northern sees. 26 of these cathedrals have a history dating back to the Middle Ages which means they were originally Roman Catholic churches and/or Benedictine and Augustinian monastery abbeys up until the 16th Century Reformation which saw England leave the Church of Rome and set up its own Protestant church with the monarch as its supreme head.

Following this split, Roman Catholics were forced to worship in secret until restrictions were eventually lifted in 1850 when they began establishing their own parallel diocese system which today numbers 20 cathedrals. Later immigration into this country from Eastern Europe has resulted in the Eastern

Orthodox Church setting up 13 further cathedrals in England with the Greek Orthodox possessing eight (of which seven are based in London), the Russian Orthodox two with the Egyptian Coptic, Ukrainian Catholic and Antiochan Orthodox one each.

To these 75 we can add 28 further ones which have lost their cathedral status for a variety of reasons. These include probably England's finest and most famous medieval church, Westminster Abbey. It was a cathedral for just ten years from 1540 before reverting to its previous role as a 'Royal Peculiar' – meaning it belongs to the English monarch and therefore does not have a diocese or a bishop. Some other former cathedrals have achieved iconic status (Bath Abbey, Lindisfarne and Glastonbury), others were established in isolated small towns and villages (Dorchester-on-Thames, Bradwell-on-Sea and Sherborne) whilst some were so obscure (Elmham, Dommoc and Lindsey) we do not know for certain exactly where they were located.

This book will therefore consider a total of 103 current and former English cathedrals. This figure excludes the 50-odd cathedrals that have been demolished over the centuries to make way for current cathedrals, the dismantled temporary or 'pro-cathedrals' used in the past before their replacement was consecrated or the half a dozen or so other religious sects in this country claiming cathedral status for their own churches.

This book will reject claims made in the past and still repeated today that our cathedrals were designed and built by supernatural beings, medieval kings, saints, bishops, abbots or monks. It will assert that our great abbeys and cathedrals are essentially no different from all other building projects: they required a reason to be built; they had to fulfil a function laid down by a client or patron, they needed a suitable site on which to be erected, adequate funding, a highly trained designer, a construction team with a wide range of appropriate skills and end users to utilise the completed building. What was undoubtedly true was that religion, vigorously supported by the state, its monarch and the church, was the driving force behind the whole process.

In order to obtain answers to the questions raised, the book will contain the following chapters:

• Location will look at the factors that influenced where English cathedrals were built and will include some historical context which affected this decision. This will cover the occupation of the country by the Romans, Anglo-Saxons and Normans; Augustine and his missionaries of 597; the split from the Church of Rome and the formation of the Protestant Anglican church in 1533/4; the closure of all of England's monasteries; the English Civil Wars and changes brought by the world's first Industrial Revolution which led to massive shifts in population in the 18th and 19th centuries.

- The Patron will investigate who commissioned the building of England's cathedrals and the organisation that they led. It will examine the power and wealth of the bishops, abbots, cathedrals and monasteries in the Middle Ages and look at the differences between the secular and monastic cathedral.

- Finance will analyse how the building of an English cathedral was funded, where the money came from and include some contemporary costs, prices and wages. It will consider why one cathedral was completed in only 46 years whilst another one took nearly 250 years to finish.

- Purpose will consider the function of the English cathedral and how this changed up to the Reformation in the 16th Century. It will start with a basic Norman cathedral plan and look at how additional space for shrines, processions, chapels and new architectural styles effected the layout, the aesthetics and the size of the cathedral.

- Design will look at who created the English cathedral, what were their influences, how were they trained and expose the myth of the religious designer and builder. It will look at design rules, geometry, duplication, competition and empiric learning as well as examining the life of a medieval architect.

- The Building investigates how the English cathedral was erected and by whom including the challenges, the organisation, the materials and the equipment. Subjects covered include the cathedral's orientation, sequence of working, transportation of materials, the building trades and will include some contemporary accounts of building operations.

- Post Completion will look at how the English cathedral has changed since it was largely completed in the late Middle Ages. This chapter covers a change of religion, the Puritan victory in the English Civil Wars, the rise of non-Conformist religions leading to cathedral neglect, damaging restoration schemes caused by a shift in architectural fashion as well as their subsequent rise in popularity.

- Conclusions will summarise the answers to the questions raised in the introduction and look at the English cathedral today.

- In the appendices,

  A) contains a glossary of any specialist terms used in this book;

  B) includes a brief description of England's 103 current and former cathedrals which have been *highlighted* thus when they first appear in chapter 2;

  C) gives a list of recommended further reading and notes on the numbers that appear in the text.

All prices and costs quoted in this book have been converted to the British pound (£/p) followed by a present day value (PDV) obtained by using standard inflation tables. This allows a monetary comparison to be made over the period covered in this book. While this is more accurate for commodity prices, wages and particularly project costs will often be as much as 35 times higher than the PDV figures for status and prestige reasons.

I have attempted to use plain English throughout this book but where this has proved impossible, for example with the use of some historical, architectural, technical and religious terms, I have included an explanation within the glossary at appendix A.

2. LOCATION
What factors influenced where English Cathedrals were built?

....

Τhe ancient cathedral city of Lincoln lies approximately halfway between the south coast of England and the Scottish border to the north yet 21 of England's 26 medieval cathedrals are located to the south whilst only Carlisle, Durham, Ripon and York are to the north. The headquarters of the Church of England and worldwide Anglican Communion is located not in London, the capital and by far the country's largest and wealthiest city, but in Canterbury in the far south-east of England. The towns of Leeds, Stoke-on-Trent, Hull, Nottingham, Sunderland, Brighton, Plymouth, Wolverhampton and Southampton all have populations of over 250,000 but have no Anglican cathedral yet six cathedrals are located in places with less than 30,000 inhabitants: Chichester, Truro, Ely, Ripon and Wells whilst Southwell has only 6,900 citizens. In the past some were built in even more remote and sparsely populated places that few people other than locals know exist. North Elmham is a small Norfolk village, Bradwell-on-Sea is a tiny Essex coastal settlement while the isolated town of Dorchester-on-Thames (current population 1,400) in rural Oxfordshire once had a diocese that stretched as far north as the river Humber. The reasons for these anomalies are the direct result of historical events going back nearly 2,000 years and forms the basis of this first chapter.

The first Christian set foot on English soil shortly after 43AD when the Romans occupied the country. St Alban, England's first Christian martyr who was murdered in the second half of the third Century, is believed to lie beneath the present cathedral in the city that still bears his name. We do know that a couple of years after the Roman Empire adopted Christianity as its official religion, three bishops from York, London and either Lincoln or Colchester, attended a meeting in Arles (France) in 314 which would indicate that Roman England had at least a basic church diocese system linked to continental Europe. Even though Roman remains have been discovered under York, Southwark, Chichester and Southwell cathedrals, finding a Roman Christian building beneath an English cathedral has remained elusive. Archaeologists have failed to find anything of Venerable Bede's Roman church below Canterbury Cathedral nor was the Roman Temple of Diana discovered when Christopher Wren's St Paul's Cathedral was being excavated in 1675. One modest-sized Roman church has, however, been unearthed at Silchester in Hampshire.

The Romans increased cultural, trade and religious links to Europe and their urban and military settlements prospered with many subsequent English cities having origins dating from this period. While London was capital of southern England and York the main town in the northern province, up to 13 other walled towns became locations of cathedrals (Bath, Canterbury, Carlisle, Chester, Chichester, Dorchester-on-Thames, Exeter, Gloucester, Leicester, Lincoln, Rochester, St Albans and Winchester). These settlements were linked by a series of major roads, Fosse and Icknield Ways, Watling, Akeman and Ermine Streets that traversed the country.

Following the Romans departure in around 410, the country was invaded and occupied by pagan Germanic tribes from north Europe: the Jutes settled in Kent, the Saxons in Wessex, Sussex, and Essex and the Angles in Mercia (the Midlands), East Anglia and Northumbria. They tended to occupy former Roman towns and created seven increasingly stable kingdoms known as the Heptarchy. The native Britons were driven into the peripheral areas of the country, to Cornwall, Wales and the north-west, with Christianity only being kept alive in these outlying regions thanks to missionaries from Ireland and Scotland. Gradually this Celtic strand of the religion was reintroduced back into the occupied areas of England with monasteries being established in remote rural locations.

A more widespread and lasting attempt to convert pagan England to Christianity came in 597 when Pope Gregory the Great's emissary, Augustine, arrived with 40 monks in south-east England to attempt to bring the country under the Church of Rome's authority. He was received by the King of Kent, Ethelbert, who gave him permission to preach his religion and donated sites in his capital, Canterbury, on which to build a church and a monastery. Ethelbert's wife Bertha, a Frankish princess, was already a Christian and used the town's *Church of St Martin (Canterbury)* which dates from the Roman era, as her private chapel. Augustine appears to have utilised this building as his mission's headquarters until a new church and monastery were built. St Martin's is still used today as a parish church and therefore has the distinction of being England's longest continually-used Christian building as well as being its oldest surviving former cathedral.

According to Bede, the original *Canterbury Cathedral* church also dates from the Roman era and was repaired circa 598-602 to become the new base for Augustine's missionaries. Not surprisingly nothing remains today of this church but fragments of a later one, probably from the middle of the 10th Century, have been discovered. It was rectangular in plan with the nave, flanked by aisles, containing a low screened off area for the choir. The raised presbytery at the east end terminated in a semi-circular apse which included the High Altar with a crypt beneath. A raised west end apse contained another altar along with the bishop's throne facing east whilst the church was entered on both sides through porches which had towers above.

Augustine also organised the building of a monastery, known as St Augustine Abbey (Canterbury), as a residence for himself and his followers which was completed in 613. The Normans completely rebuilt the settlement after their Conquest in 1066 and it remained a monastery until it was closed, sold and largely demolished as part of the Reformation in 1538. What remains of this settlement can be visited today, courtesy of English Heritage.

Ethelbert allowed Augustine to set up another base in his Kent kingdom and so *Rochester Cathedral* was established in 604. The church from this era was discovered following excavations around the west end of the current cathedral in 1888. This measures 17.3 metres in length and 9.3 metres in width and consists of a rectangular nave terminating via a triple archway in a full-width circular apse at the east end. The plan of this church has been marked out on the ground in and next to the present cathedral.

The East Saxons lived in the adjoining kingdom of Essex which was also overseen by Ethelbert who gave consent in 604 for a third see to be created with its cathedral located in its most important town, London. It is thought the original *London - St Paul's Cathedral* was erected on the present site, being the highest point in the City of London. Unsurprisingly, nothing remains above ground of this church or the three subsequent ones which were all destroyed by fires in 962, 1087 and, most famously, in 1666. In around 616 the first Bishop of London Mellitus, was expelled from the city following the death of the Christian supporting king, with the religion not returning to London until around 675. Rochester suffered a similar fate and both bishops were forced to flee to France. Bishop Laurence of Canterbury, however, managed to hold onto his seat, so retaining the Church of Rome's fragile presence in this country. It had always been Augustine's intention to move the archbishopric of England to London but this sixty year period of religious uncertainty meant that it stayed in the more stable city of Canterbury. Today Canterbury Cathedral is still the headquarters of the Anglican Church, the result of events that took place around 1,400 years ago.

The expulsion of the Christian church from London meant that an alternative refuge was required and this came in the unlikely form of a disused Roman fort on the Essex coast. *Bradwell-on-Sea - St. Peter-on-the-Wall* church was built as a temporary replacement and served as the seat for the Bishop of London from about 654 until c675. Subsequently abandoned, it was used as a barn before being restored and re-consecrated in 1920. Much reduced in size, the church is still used as a chapel and is open to the public.

Following Augustine's death in 604, Paulinus his successor was invited by Ethelbert's Christian daughter to baptise her husband, Edwin, the king of Northumbria. This resulted in England's first northern see being established in *York* in 627. A modest timber church was erected on the site of a former Roman fort but this was soon replaced by a 'larger, nobler, basilica of stone.' The settlement lasted only briefly before the Northumbrians were defeated by the pagan Mercian's in around 633. Two years later, when Oswald became king of Northumbria, he invited the Celtic monk Aidan to convert his subjects to Christianity and he established his bishopric in the monastery at *Lindisfarne,* an island off the north-east coast of Northumberland.

The approach used by these pioneering Christian missionaries to spread their religion was repeated elsewhere. Paulinus entered *Lindsey* (present day Lincolnshire) and probably founded a bishopric in the Roman city of Lincoln in around 628 before expanding into East Anglia with a cathedral being established possibly first at *Soham* before it was transferred to *Dommoc* in 630. A see in Wessex was founded at *Dorchester-on-Thames* in 635 before moving to *Winchester* in around 660 while Mercia was created, possibly initially at *Repton* in 655, before being relocated to *Lichfield* in 669. The expansion and retention of Christianity in these early years was, as we have seen in London and York, entirely dependent on royal patronage and their religious preference.

In 664 a Synod held in Whitby established the dominance of the Church of Rome over the Celtic strand which subsequently withdrew to Iona (Scotland), with Roman Catholicism becoming the principal faith of the English until its split with Rome in 1533. A new church administrator Theodore of Tarsus (603-690) arrived in the country in 669 and found the church in disarray with no bishops in Wessex, Mercia, East Anglia or Rochester. Within three years he re-drew the diocese map of England creating new cathedrals in East Anglia at *Elmham* in about 673; in Northumbria at *Hexham* in 680 and *Ripon* in about 686; in Mercia at *Hereford*, *Leicester* and *Worcester* in c679; in Sussex at *Selsey* in 681 and, after his death, in Wessex at *Sherborne* in 705.

After 793, England suffered increasingly from attacks from marauding Viking raiders from Norway and Denmark. By 865 Danish invaders had occupied East Anglia, two years later they captured Northumbria, including its capital York, and in 875 Mercia was conquered which left a third of the country under their control in what became known as 'Danelaw.' In the early years of the 10th Century, the Vikings also colonised the northern part of France

(Normannia / Normandy – the land of the Norseman). They quickly evolved, converting to Christianity, learning French, marrying into their royal family, taking French titles and established a region which rivalled the rest of France in terms of wealth and power.

Christianity was severely weakened, particularly in Eastern England, by these pagan raiders from northern Europe. Churches and monasteries were destroyed and vacated, monks slaughtered, their treasures and books looted. In the north, Hexham and Lindisfarne were abandoned in around 875 whilst York was impoverished. The monks from Lindisfarne took the body of their former Bishop Cuthbert and their treasures, establishing themselves briefly in *Chester-le-Street* in around 883 before finally settling in *Durham* in 995. Further south, Dommoc, Elmham, Lindsey and Leicester were abandoned and their sees were taken over in circa 870 by Dorchester-on-Thames in the safer environs of rural Oxfordshire with its massive diocese now stretching over 150 miles from the rivers Thames to the Humber. In the more stable south-west England, four more dioceses were created: first from around 865-900 at either *Bodmin* or Launceston (present day Cornwall) before it was moved onto either *St Germans* or Bodmin in circa 930; in 909 three cathedrals were founded at *Wells* (Somerset), *Crediton* (Devon) and *Ramsbury* (Wiltshire). Two East Anglian sees were established in the isolated villages of *Hoxne* in Suffolk in c950 closely followed by the re-establishment of the Elmham bishopric, most probably at *North Elmham* (Norfolk) in around 955. Only fragments of these Anglo-Saxon cathedrals survive although amazingly the 7th Century crypts at Ripon and Hexham remain intact beneath later churches. Some masonry from the period has been found in the parish church at Dorchester-on-Thames whilst excavations beneath Exeter, Peterborough, St Albans, Wells, Winchester and Worcester cathedrals have revealed the remains of churches from this pre-Norman period.

The resistance to Viking incursions was led by various Anglo-Saxon monarchs, most successfully by Alfred the Great (849-99), King of Wessex, who managed to drive them out of East Anglia, Mercia and finally Northumbria by 954. He is credited with unifying England (Engla lond – 'land of the Angles') for the first time which resulted in a more stable country. This led to a proliferation of monasteries under Dunstan with services and rituals being standardised based on the Benedictine monastic order imported from southern Italy. Unfortunately this state of affairs was not to last with the Scandinavians launching a large scale invasion in 1013 which led to Cnut and his two sons ruling England from 1016-42. The native Anglo-Saxon dynasty was restored again in 1042 when Edward the Confessor was crowned king. Norman by education and upbringing, he introduced Continental ideas into the court, church and architecture which resulted in the rebuilding of Westminster Abbey in a Romanesque style from 1045. It was at the time by far the largest church ever built in England and was estimated to have cost him one third of his entire wealth. Minor adjustments were made to the diocese map at this time which included moving the see of Devon and Cornwall from Crediton to *Exeter* in 1050.

After allegedly promising the English crown to his Norman relations, Edward appears to have changed his mind on his death bed in 1066 and named Harold, the native Earl of Wessex, as his successor. This decision led to two rivals for the crown invading the country with Harold Hardraade, the King of Norway, first being defeated at Stamford Bridge (Yorkshire). Three days later the Normans arrived on the south coast resulting in the battle of Hastings fought on 14th October, 1066 which saw William of Normandy defeat Harold, abruptly ending the Anglo-Saxon dynasty forever.

William immediately set about dispossessing the native landowners and giving the confiscated land to his loyal Norman barons and religious acolytes in return for military service and rent. Anglo-Saxon leaders and rulers of both government and the church were similarly replaced with the resulting uprisings being ruthlessly crushed. The conquerors reinforced their power and authority with a massive military building programme involving the erection of numerous castles and fortifications in strategic cities and towns throughout the realm.

As part of this process, Lanfranc of Bec, a Benedictine monk and the Bishop of Caen, was appointed Archbishop of Canterbury in 1070 and he set about re-organising the English church on Continental lines. The five rural cathedrals that existed at the time were transferred to more easily defended towns. Mercia's massive see was moved from Dorchester-on-Thames to *Lincoln* in c1075 and the bishopric of East Anglia was transferred from North Elmham, first to *Thetford* and then onto *Norwich* in c1094. It is believed the original intention was to move this to the great abbey and monastery of Bury St Edmunds but it was discovered that an early episcopal charter preventing this could not be overturned. In 1075 Lichfield, Selsey and Sherborne sees were relocated to *Chester Collegiate Church, Chichester* and *Old Sarum* (Salisbury) respectively.

These five new cathedrals along with the ten existing ones (starting at Canterbury, continuing with Rochester, Winchester, Hereford, Worcester, Durham, Exeter, St Paul's London, York and Wells) and other significant monasteries (St Albans, Ely, Gloucester, and Peterborough) were all completely rebuilt in the century following the Conquest. Their Anglo-Saxon predecessors were ruthlessly swept away to be replaced by churches built on an unprecedented scale in the new Romanesque style equal to anything found in Europe.

The 10th Century monastic revival had introduced a concept to England found in only one other place in Europe (Sicily), the monastic cathedral. In this arrangement the bishop's seat was accommodated inside the monastery's abbey with the ordained monks providing him with more ordered support. The bishop was, as usual, the head of the diocese becoming the monasteries titular abbot while a prior was put in charge of the monastery and its monks. This occurred at Canterbury, Sherborne, Winchester and Worcester in the Anglo-Saxon period and Lanfranc extended this by adding Benedictine monasteries to Durham, Rochester and Norwich cathedrals. This also occurred at *Ely* and *Carlisle* when they both became cathedrals in 1109 and in around 1133 respectively. This system, however, lead to supremacy disputes between the bishop and the prior with the Pope frequently being called in to adjudicate. Occasionally this resulted in the bishop moving his seat out of the abbey into another church which meant that the diocese had joint cathedrals. In around 1102 the bishopric at Chester was moved to *Coventry* but in 1189 a serious disagreement occurred between monastic Coventry and secular Lichfield, with neither being able to establish outright control of the diocese. The dispute continued until it was finally agreed in 1248 that the bishopric would be held jointly by both cathedrals, a situation that continued until 1539 when it reverted solely to Lichfield. Even more tortuous was the diocese of Somerset after the bishopric was moved from Wells to *Bath* in 1090. It was subsequently jointly held between Bath and *Glastonbury* from about 1195 to 1218, then shared between Bath and Wells from 1245 until 1539 after which Wells became the sole cathedral although the diocese is still known today as Bath and Wells.

The Normans, who helped expel occupying Muslims from Sicily, Italy and Southern Spain, were an integral member of the European Christian crusades to Palestine from 1095 onwards in an attempt to recover the Holy Land from Saracen control. These campaigns resulted in hundreds of Arabs being taken prisoners-of-war, many of whom were shipped back to France. Some were military engineers with highly developed skills gained in the Middle East of the pointed arch, dome and elaborate ceiling vaulting, elements that formed the basis of Gothic ecclesiastical architecture. Indeed without Islamic and Byzantine know-how, it would not have been possible to build the large medieval cathedrals of France and England.

The bulky Romanesque masonry with small windows giving gloomy cathedral interiors were soon deemed obsolete when compared with the more slender, delicate Gothic stonework which allowed for larger windows, producing brighter, better lit churches. Between 1189 and 1558 most of England's medieval cathedrals were rebuilt either partly or completely in the new Gothic style with its four English sub-divisions: Early English, Decorated, Perpendicular and Tudor. Once again Canterbury was first to experience the new style when the French master mason William of Sens rebuilt the east end of the cathedral following a fire in 1174. This led to a second wave of intense church building activity which lasted until the mid-13th Century and involved the rebuilding of Lincoln, Wells and York cathedrals whilst others (Chichester, Lichfield, Rochester, Southwell, Winchester and Worcester) had their east ends reconfigured. This was helped by the increased wealth of cathedrals brought about by higher rents, taxes and income from the expanding wool trade.

The new style was fully demonstrated in the building of *Salisbury* Cathedral. It was decided in 1219 that the Old Sarum site was unsuitable because of its exposed location, lack of adequate water supply and problems caused by its close proximity to a military fort. Its replacement was built in just 46 years two miles away on a greenfield site and, uniquely for a medieval English cathedral, in a single architectural style – Early English. Other than the addition of its iconic steeple and some later controversial restoration works, it stands today as it was completed in 1266.

A third wave of cathedral building continued well into the middle of the 14th Century, probably peaking in around the year 1300, resulting in more elaborate, delicate designs particularly in window tracery and column heads. Cathedrals were described at the time as being awash with money. Exeter Cathedral was almost completely rebuilt during this period while grander east ends required to house larger more elaborate shrines and memorials were undertaken at Durham, Ely, Gloucester, Lincoln, St Albans and Wells cathedrals.

England endured a series of bubonic plagues, commonly known as the Black Death, the most serious of which occurred from 1348-51. Up to a third of its estimated three million population died, with closed communities like monasteries suffering even higher fatality rates. The plague resulted in severe labour shortages, a decline in religious faith and belief in the established church. The church became even more unpopular because of its support for the introduction of poll taxes to fund a war with France which led to the Peasants Revolt in south-east England in 1381. Cathedrals, abbeys and their personnel were attacked and even murdered. This unpopularity was articulated by John Wycliffe (c1330-84) and his followers, the Lollards, who criticised the wealth and dogma of the Catholic Church and believed that Christians should be able to read the Bible themselves in their own language. It took until 1530 before William Tyndale (c1492-1536) translated the book into English, so finally breaking the church's monopoly on its interpretation. England became embroiled in a royal succession conflict known as the 'Wars of the Roses' which was fought between the Houses of York and Lancaster in 1455-87 with the Yorkist Richard III being killed in the decisive battle of the war at Bosworth Field (Leicestershire) in 1485. Incredibly, in 2012 his lost remains were discovered buried in a public car park close to Leicester Cathedral. DNA tests conclusively identified his body and he was given a more fitting internment in the nearby cathedral in March 2015.

Only one further English cathedral was erected in the late Middle Ages. Bath Abbey was rebuilt in the early part of the 16th Century but on a far more modest scale being only half the length of its Norman predecessor. The diocese map of England at the time had remained unchanged since c1228 and was far from being satisfactory: the sees were unequal in size; some were exceptionally large with their cathedrals located at their periphery and were based more on Anglo-Saxon kingdoms than contemporary regions and populations. The Pope gave King Henry VIII (1509-47) permission to close some smaller monasteries and use the money raised to reform the dioceses by creating up to 18 new cathedrals. This reorganisation never occurred as a power struggle developed between Rome and Henry following his desire to annul one marriage and legitimise another. This was to culminate in 1533/4 with England leaving the Catholic community and forming an independent Church of England with the king as its head. This schism, known as the English Reformation, also brought in new Protestant ideas from northern Europe which were at odds with traditional Catholic beliefs and were to lead to the widespread destruction of English church buildings, their fixtures and fittings.

In order to reduce the perceived threat to the new church that the monasteries posed by remaining loyal to Rome as well as raising much needed money for the cash strapped Royal Treasury, Henry's advisers proposed that all the country's monasteries, nunneries and friaries be closed. The subsequent 'Dissolution of the Monasteries' Acts of Parliament resulted in them all being shut down between 1536 and 1541 with their lands, buildings and fixtures being sold off, stripped and looted. Some magnificent religious edifices were partly or completely destroyed: the abbeys at Fountains and Rievaulx (Yorkshire), Glastonbury, Waltham (London) and the cathedrals at Leicester and Osney to name but six. All monastic cathedrals were re-constituted to be served by secular clergy while six former monastic abbey churches at *Bristol*, *Chester*, *Gloucester*, *Peterborough* and *Osney* became cathedrals. Osney's cathedral status lasted only four years before its bishop's seat was transferred to nearby *Oxford* and its wealthy estate was seized by the Crown. The sixth, *London - Westminster Abbey*, was also made into a cathedral but this arrangement lasted for only ten years until 1550 before it reverted back to the monarch's ownership. It undoubtedly owed its survival, along with most of its associated monastic buildings, thanks largely to royal patronage, being the venue for all of the country's coronations from 1066 to the present day.

The English Civil Wars (1642-51) were fought between forces loyal to King Charles I and his Parliamentarians, who wanted to reduce the monarch's absolute power. Defeat resulted in the king's execution in 1649 with England becoming a republic or 'Commonwealth' under Oliver Cromwell and his son Richard. This victory unleashed another wave of iconoclasm on cathedrals in which yet more of their land was confiscated to raise money for the Parliamentarians 'New Model Army.' Hated features like Lady Chapels, cloisters, monastic buildings, rood screens, stained glass windows, statues, wall paintings and the relics of saints were all ruthlessly destroyed. In 1651 their proposal to pull down all of England's cathedrals and use the money for poor relief was only narrowly defeated in a Parliamentary debate.

The monarchy was restored in 1660 which was widely celebrated by the English Church. Just six years later the Great Fire of London destroyed much of the city including Old St Paul's Cathedral which was rebuilt in just 35 years by Sir Christopher Wren starting in 1675 in a classical Renaissance style with an untraditional, iconic dome. It was the first purpose-built Anglican Cathedral to be constructed in this country.

The apathy shown towards cathedrals and Gothic architecture in particular continued into the mid-19th Century resulting in neglect and severe decay. Many suffered as a result of unsympathetic restoration projects while St Albans and Winchester cathedrals were in such a poor state of repair they were threatened with demolition. Increased tourism caused by the arrival of the railway age in the Victorian era led to a revival of interest in England's medieval cathedrals and resulted in their widespread restoration.

England became the world's first Industrial country from the mid-18th Century with manufacturing being undertaken by machinery rather than by hand in large factory units which resulted in enormous population shifts from the countryside to towns. The new demographics of the period, particularly affecting the north of England and the Midlands, saw major changes to the diocese map which had remained unchanged for 294 years. Twenty new cathedrals were created: four old foundation churches at *Ripon* (re-established in 1836 after a break of some 1,150 years), *St Albans* (1877), *Southwell Minster* (1884) and *London - Southwark* (1905) were raised in status; 12 former parish churches at *Birmingham* (1905), *Blackburn* (1926), *Bradford* (1919), *Bury St Edmunds* (1914), *Chelmsford* (1914), *Derby* (1927), *Leicester* (1927), *Manchester* (1847), *Newcastle* (1882), *Portsmouth* (1927), *Sheffield* (1914) and *Wakefield* (1888) became cathedrals; four new ones were erected first at *Truro* (began in 1876, opened 1910), *Guildford* (started in 1927, opened 1961), *Coventry* (a former parish church was used from 1918 before it was completely destroyed during the Second World War with its replacement opening in 1962) and finally *Liverpool* (commenced in 1880, fully completed 1978).

Those wishing to continue with their Roman Catholic faith were forced to do so discreetly for fear of persecution and death. The Catholic Emancipation Act of 1829 slowly eased these restrictions but it was not until 1850 that a Roman Catholic diocesan system could be finally established. Today this comprises of 19 dioceses with 20 cathedrals found at *Arundel* (diocese established in 1965), *Birmingham* (1850), *Brentwood* (1917), *Clifton, Bristol* (1850), *Lancaster* (1924), *Leeds* (1878), *Liverpool* (1850), *London Westminster* and *Southwark* (both 1850), *Middlesbrough* (1878), *Newcastle-upon-Tyne* (1850), *Northampton* (1850), *Norwich* (1976), *Nottingham* (1850), *Plymouth* (1850), *Portsmouth* (1882), *Salford, Greater Manchester* (1850), *Hallam, Sheffield* (1980) and *Shrewsbury* (1850). A cathedral for the Roman Catholic Bishop of the Forces was created at *Aldershot* (1972).

To cater for immigrants from Eastern Europe, the first Greek Orthodox Church was opened in London as early as the 17th Century with a Russian one following a century later. Today there are 13 Eastern Orthodox cathedrals in England with Greek ones based in *Birmingham* (cathedral established in 1958) and seven in *London at Camberwell* (1977), *Camden* (1991), *Golders Green* (1979), *Kentish Town* (1970), *Shepherd's Bush* (1963), *Bayswater, Westminster* (1922) and *Wood Green* (1985). London also hosts Russian Orthodox cathedrals at *Chiswick* (1999) and *Kensington* (1956), a Ukrainian one at *Mayfair* (1968) and an Antiochian one in *Regent's Park* (1989). There is also an Egyptian Coptic Orthodox cathedral in *Stevenage* (2002).

In an effort to save money and rationalise the sees of Yorkshire to more closely align with the population of the area, it was decided in 2014 to merge

Bradford, Wakefield and Ripon to create the new diocese of West Yorkshire and the Dales under the Bishop of Leeds, the first change to England's ecclesiastical map since 1927. The former cathedrals in the area will retain their status for the time being and it is anticipated that as part of this process Leeds Minster will eventually be given cathedral status.

3. THE PATRON

Who commissioned the building of England's Cathedrals?

....

T he patrons who commissioned the building of England's cathedrals and abbeys in the Middle Ages following the Norman Conquest were the bishops and abbots, the leaders of the cathedrals, dioceses and the monasteries. Today they would be known as the client being responsible for finding a site, setting the budget, raising the finance, appointing a competent designer and assisting with the project brief which sets out how the building should function and perform. They were likely to hold strong views on how their new edifice should look based on completed schemes which they had visited, read or heard about.

Bishops and abbots were rich and powerful men, living a lifestyle similar to the country's gentry. As well as having a palace within the cathedral precincts, they were also likely to possess fine country houses, castles, large rural estates and mansions in central London where their names survive to this day: Lincoln's Inn, Ely Place and Whitehall, the site of the Archbishop of York's palace[1]. From these residences and estates, bishops and abbots were able to entertain visitors and guests including royalty in lavish style. When Edward II visited Peterborough in the early 14th Century it allegedly cost the monastery £1,543 (PDV £1.27 million) to entertain him. In return and like all landowners in a feudal society, they were under an obligation to provide the Crown with a set number of knights and men-at-arms who also acted as ecclesiastic bodyguards.

A bishop's role in medieval society extended far beyond their religious duties with several becoming high ranking government officials. Bishop Courtenay of Norwich, for example, was so busy undertaking his duties as Treasurer to the Royal Household that he never managed to pay a single visit to his cathedral, let alone his diocese. In the Middle Ages, England's 17 bishops and 27 abbots from the so-called 'mitred abbeys' were an inherent part of the Establishment being entitled to sit in the House of Lords, the upper chamber of the Houses of Parliament. Even today 26 unelected Anglican archbishops and bishops still retain their seats influencing the way the country is governed, a situation only replicated elsewhere in the world in Iran. It was hardly surprising then that they became embroiled in political disputes and military action. Simon of Sudbury, the Archbishop of Canterbury, who, as Chancellor of England proposed the hated poll tax which led to the Peasants Revolt, was beheaded in the Tower of London in June 1381 for his part in the conflict.

There were two types of cathedral in Middle Age England: the monastic and the secular cathedral. Monasteries were generally the larger establishment, isolated from the local community with all except their leaders sharing communal accommodation. The secular cathedral on the other hand was run by clergy who did not take monastic vows, lived in their own houses and, as the name suggests, were far more involved with the outside world. Initially it was the monasteries who were the innovators of Norman church design before the great secular cathedrals at Lincoln, Salisbury, Wells and York developed the Gothic architectural style when it arrived later in England.

In both establishments, bishops, abbots and priors were assisted by a chapter of prelates, who were responsible for running the cathedral on a day-to-day basis. A member of the chapter was frequently tasked with undertaking the patron's role being known as the 'keeper of the fabric' and responsible for controlling the cathedral's building budget. The chapter member frequently appointed was the sacrist, the keeper of the cathedral's treasures. So when secular Salisbury Cathedral was built in the 13th Century and monastic Ely's central tower collapsed a century later to be replaced by the extraordinary timber octagon, both employed their sacrists, Elias de Dereham and Alan de Walsingham respectively, to undertake the role of 'keeper of the fabric.' Specialist design and construction issues were handled by a layman, the 'master of the works' mostly a master stonemason. Their two roles and responsibilities frequently overlapped which has created much subsequent misunderstanding[2].

The Monastic Cathedral

The first monasteries were established in England by monks from Ireland and Scotland but it was Augustine who first introduced the Benedictine Order into the country. St Benedict had founded a monastery at Monte Casino in southern Italy in 529 with his rules becoming universally adopted throughout Western Europe with Church of Rome support. They were known as the 'Black Monks' because of the colour of their clothing, giving vows of poverty, chastity and obedience with all possessions being held in common. Monasteries initially focused solely on prayer, study and self-sufficiency but this was to radically change as they became more involved with external business and commerce.

Waves of other monastic and religious orders followed often reinforcing the original Benedictines beliefs and rules. The Cistercians or 'white monks' arrived in England in 1128, seeking isolated sites in which to practice their extreme austere regime, for example by refusing to wear warm clothes or shoes. The order helped to cultivate some of England's most barren and isolated landscapes, characteristics which were to prevent any of their abbey's becoming cathedrals with the haunting ruins at Rievaulx and Fountains Abbeys in Yorkshire bearing ample testimony. In contrast, six priories served by Augustinian 'Black Canons regular' who undertook pastoral and monastic duties in more urban locations, eventually become cathedrals (Bristol, Carlisle, Osney, Oxford, Portsmouth and Southwark). These monastic orders were followed in the 13th Century by the friars or preaching orders who were inspired by the teachings of Francis of Assisi (1181-1224). Their simple lifestyle and plain, prosaic churches, however, had little impact on England's cathedral narrative.

On the eve of the Norman Conquest, England had about 50 monasteries and 12 nunneries served by some 1,000 monks and nuns, owning approximately 17% of the country's land. Their popularity increased enormously with Norman support so that by their 13th Century zenith there were some 800 religious houses served by around 20,000[3] monks and nuns out of a total population of around three million. St Albans was the country's largest monastery having about 100 monks whilst Durham, Winchester, Norwich, Peterborough and Glastonbury all had over 60. When lay-brothers and servants were taken into account, the total community could be over three times these numbers. The bubonic plague in the late 14th Century had a huge impact on some monasteries with St Albans losing its abbot and 47 monks while at Westminster Abbey the abbot and 26 monks perished. In contrast, Canterbury lost just four monks, probably because of its better hygiene standards.

The primary duty of monks was to participate in and attend the eight daily services, the so called *Opus Dei,* 'the work of God.' A monks' day was divided into 12 canonical hours between sunrise and sunset so each hour varied depending on the time of year; 90 minutes in summer to only 40 in winter. At the two equinoxes (when the length of daylight equalled the hours of darkness) their timetable of services commenced with the Virgils service followed by meditation at 2am; at first light Lauds was followed at 6am by Prime; 9am was Terce (the third hour); 12noon Sext (the sixth hour); 3pm Nones (the ninth hour); 4.30pm Vespers (named after the evening star) and finally at 6pm (dusk) Compline. These services therefore necessitated at least seven separate visits to the abbey's choir where monks stood, knelt or perched on misericords while services were read and chanted unaccompanied by any form of music.

Monks also had an obligation to attend other services that might well involve a daily mass to the Virgin Mary in the Lady Chapel and the singing of soul masses at the numerous chantry chapels and shrines. The repetitive nature of their daily routine was broken up by Sunday's, annual festivals particularly at

Easter and Christmas, the numerous Saint Days, royal visits, funerals and enthronements. These events would invariably involve music, spectacular and colourful processions through the adjoining town, the cathedral's precincts and the nave with the sprinkling of holy water on altars before the celebration of high mass in the abbey's choir.

Monks other duties were fitted in around the requirements of *Opus Dei*. Following Terce at 9am, they were required to attend a meeting in the chapter house which was usually a significant architectural feature in the monastery being either circular, octagonal or polygonal in shape. Business started with a reading of a chapter of the monastery's rule book, hence the building's name, followed by a commemoration of the saint of the day and any obituaries. The agenda would typically include monastery business, problems and disputes involving rents on their land and properties, followed by any confessions with punishments being imposed by the attending senior prelate. The one meal of the day was taken after Sext at noon which, in the summer, was followed by a short siesta. Other manual, literacy and administration duties were fitted in around this timetable and might involve washing, cooking, gardening, domestic service, teaching, music, writing, studying, copying, illustrating and maintaining books or carving, painting and making jewellery.

There were seven grades of monk which started at novice level and progressed to doorkeeper, exorcist, reader, acolyte, sub-deacon and deacon which was priest status. He could rise further into various specialist roles known as obedientaries. These prelates were responsible for managing the various monastic departments and could number between 15 and 20 depending on the size of the establishment. They would typically include the bishop, abbot or prior, the precentor (who oversaw the music); the receiver (who acted as the treasurer auditing all incoming and outgoing revenues); the cellarer (who supplied the food and drink); the sacrist (the keeper of church relics, ornaments, vestments, bibles and order of service); the refectorarian (who maintained the dining hall), the chamberlain (responsible for clothing, shoes and bedding); infirmarer (who ran the hospital) and the almoner (who gave money, clothing and food to the needy). Norwich Cathedral, for example, gave away between 240 and 275 loaves of bread every day as well as clothes, shoes, ale, meat, fish, eggs and peat for fuel to the local poor.

A monastery's wide-range of functions necessitated many communal buildings and a standardised monastic plan developed. At its heart were the cloisters which, as well as providing a glazed, covered passageway linking all the major buildings, was also used for studying, writing and other sedentary activities. Built around an open quadrangle or garth it was normally sited on the warmer south side of the abbey off which were typically the chapter house, the communal dormitory (or dorter) with adjoining reredorter (communal lavatories), the refectory (frater) for eating with an adjacent kitchen. The frater had a raised platform for the obedientaries with monks sitting in rows of tables at right angles. Near its entrance door would be the lavatorium containing a trough with running water for washing hands and faces prior to eating. Meals were accompanied by ale and wine and eaten in silence except for one monk reading from the scriptures or giving a sermon.

The cathedral precinct also contained a number of other buildings like the bishop's palace, private houses for the abbot or the prior, a guest house, prison, accommodation for lay-brothers and servants, laundries, workshops, cellars, various barns and stores. Some cathedrals, notably Canterbury, Durham, Hereford, Peterborough and York, possessed libraries to match anything found elsewhere in the country. Even today Lincoln and Salisbury cathedrals possess two of the four surviving copies of the Magna Carta while Hereford has the Mappa Mundi, a 13th Century religious map of the world. The monastery was, as far as possible, self-sufficient producing their own bread, meat, grain, butter, honey, ale, wine, herbs, fruit and vegetables. The infirmary (hospital) usually had its own chapel and kitchen and, along with the warming house and main kitchen, was the only other heated monastic building.

It is important to emphasise that monasteries were not welcoming, open public buildings. Their prime duty was to offer continuous prayers to God and to the souls of the departed with their services being conducted exclusively by monks and priests. They undertook no pastoral work within the local community whatsoever for which the local parish church was deemed solely responsible. Any attending members of the public (they could hardly be described as being part of a congregation) were there solely to listen, not participate in the rituals being performed in private behind screens in the east end of the abbey church.

The Secular Cathedral

The monastic and secular cathedrals had similarities. They both observed the same canonical hours, the *Opus Dei* and, initially at least, their clergy lived communally. The secular canons, however, gradually acquired individual income from property or land, known as a prebend, which enabled them to move into their own property adjoining the cathedral. The most complete surviving precincts can be found at Salisbury and Wells which includes the Vicars' Close, Bishops Palace, Deanery and other residences. Secular cathedrals tended to be served by nearly as many clergy as monasteries; Lincoln Cathedral had 58 clerics, Salisbury 52, York 36, Lichfield 32 and St Paul's 30.

As with the monastic cathedral, the bishop was seldom present, only attending major festivals, enthronements or funerals. A dean headed the secular establishment again assisted by a chapter of canons made up of a precentor (responsible for services, the choir and the music school), a chancellor (in charge of education and scholarships), a treasurer (responsible not for the cathedral's finances but for the library, the archives, sacred ornaments and objects), a sacrist (the treasurer's assistant) and a number of archdeacons who assisted the bishop in running the diocese.

Many secular canons obtained other paid work outside of the cathedral in local parish churches, law courts and the universities which often resulted in the mother church being poorly served. To overcome this problem some larger cathedrals began employing so called singing vicars (from the term vicarious – filling the place of another). In others, canons were offered additional money to attend services which sometimes led to them becoming increasingly wealthy. This can be illustrated by the fact that clerics at Lichfield Cathedral were required to donate £66 annually (PDV £50,600) to the dean and spend £40 a year (£30,600) to entertain church and local dignitaries, this when the subsistence level at the time was just £6 a year (PDV £4,600).

The extensive communal buildings seen in monasteries were not strictly required in secular establishments although cloisters were added to Salisbury in c1263-94 and to Old St Paul's from 1332. In 1285 the precentor of Exeter Cathedral was murdered returning from a 2am service while the precincts at Lincoln Cathedral were described as being full of desperadoes who were a menace to the personal safety of the clergy. This led to the majority of both monastic and secular cathedrals being surrounded by walls and gatehouses with fine surviving examples to be found at Bristol, Bury St Edmunds, Canterbury, Peterborough and St Albans. The gatehouse at Ely dating from c1396 has been variously used as a prison, chapel and brewery before its current usage as a school.

The church in the Middle Ages had their own laws and courts to deal with disputes that arose because of their considerable property and land interests. This did not always prevent trouble arising as townsfolk and trade guilds tried to break free of the imposed taxes and restrictions - Norwich priory was burnt down in 1272 whilst St Albans suffered serious rioting in 1327. The church was also responsible for arbitrating on all moral issues. In 1510/1 Norwich Cathedral court met on no fewer than 65 occasions, with sentences ranging from public humiliation to excommunication. A number of English cathedrals also possessed the right of sanctuary which gave those seeking it freedom from being arrested if they kept within a defined area for a period of time - at York this was 30 days whilst at Durham it was 27[4].

Literacy was not thought to be an essential requirement for life until universal education was introduced in England in 1870, before which pictorial windows, wall paintings, graphic sculptures and miracle plays were the means used to communicate with the illiterate. At first only religious personnel were taught to read and write with both cathedrals and monasteries establishing schools to train young clerics and monks. Some of the more academic of these progressed onto the country's first universities at Oxford and Cambridge which were founded in the early Middle Ages. It was hardly surprising then, in an age when monarchs and the nobility could barely sign their names, that educated religious personnel became highly sought after to act as government officers and international diplomats. These early religious schools eventually expanded to take in children of the wealthy and were to develop into grammar schools. Later almonry schools were started for the less fortunate to provide elementary education in return for helping around the cathedral. These were often provided by wealthy benefactors who gave accommodation and an endowment to pay for a teacher. It can therefore be justifiably claimed that cathedrals and monasteries were the pioneers of the present-day education system in this country.

4. FINANCE
How was the building of the English Cathedral funded?

....

England in the Middle Ages was an agricultural society with wealth based almost exclusively on land ownership. Some 20 years after the Norman Conquest in 1066 it was estimated that just over half of the country's land was owned by fewer than 180 French barons as a reward for supporting William I's military campaign. Over half of the remaining land (26% of the total) was in the hands of the church with cathedrals and the monasteries owning large tracts of agricultural land, manors, villages and entire towns, often miles away from their base. York Minster possessed land in Hampshire and Gloucestershire, Winchester Cathedral owned Weymouth while Canterbury Cathedral held Sandwich. Large areas of the cities of Wells, Bath and Salisbury belonged to their cathedrals whilst some 30 monasteries possessed the entire borough outside their precinct as was the case at Bury St Edmunds, Coventry, Durham, Glastonbury, Peterborough and St Albans. Wealthy benefactors were to further increase this holding so that the church eventually owned one-third of all of England's land which financed the massive cathedral and abbey building programme throughout the Middle Ages.

As well as collecting rent from properties and land they owned, landowners also levied a tax on markets, fairs, roads, ale, milling, timber, fishing and game. In 1308, Durham Cathedral's revenue from land peaked at £4,526 a year only to fall to £1,212 (PDV from £3.73 million to £920,000) following the bubonic plague in the late 14th Century. In lieu of monetary rent, monastery landowners frequently received an agreed proportion of agricultural produce they did not produce themselves; for example fodder for horses, leather, timber and peat for fuel. Sheep farming became an increasing source of wealth as highly-prized English wool was exported to the European market particularly from the Cistercian monasteries of Yorkshire and Lincolnshire where the land tended to be unsuitable for arable farming. In 1086 Ely Cathedral possessed over 13,000 sheep while 300 years later it was reported that many of Norwich's 4,000 flock grazed in the cloisters.

The obligation to give 10% of the 'fruits of the land' to the local parish church was an ancient Anglo-Saxon requirement which was adopted by the Normans and lasted in England well into the 19th Century. These so-called tithes were a legal obligation imposed on the land irrespective of the landowner's class, sex or religion and were used to maintain parish churches as well as paying for their priests or presbyters. It was common for cathedrals and monasteries to hold considerable numbers of these prized parish tithes - St Albans for example held 20 and made a considerable profit in the process.

The importance of religion in medieval England to all social classes can be illustrated by the money, time and labour they all gave to the church. The wealthy put huge financial resources into enriching their local cathedrals and churches in the late Middle Ages, sponsoring new extensions, chapels, memorials and fittings. Some also gave lump sums in return for lodgings, food, drink and heat using monasteries as a kind of retirement home in their later years of life.

Nationwide appeals were often launched to fund major building projects. Old St Paul's appeal for a new east end received donations from as far afield as Norwich, Coventry, Lichfield, Ely and Salisbury. Collection boxes tended to raise only modest amounts of money. The congregation of Exeter Cathedral are said to have given £2 a year (PDV £1,530) whilst those at Ely donated a total of £16 (PDV £12,250) to the £2,046 (PDV £1.63 million) cost of erecting the octagon tower. This was hardly surprising as parishioners tended to be far more loyal and generous in giving to their parish churches which they perceived as being far more relevant to their lives than their remote cathedral or abbey.

The church taught that anyone breaking their rules would be required to serve a period of penance before being absolved of the penalty. This could last up to 20 years during which time the offender might have to sit apart in church, wear special clothes or exist on a diet of bread and water. Eventually a money-making alternative was introduced known as an indulgence whereby the wrong-doer could make a donation to reduce the penalty period. This proved a lucrative source of income for the church but the system was open to abuse and became the subject of much ridicule from opponents of the Catholic Church.

Another important revenue stream came from donations from the thousands of visitors and pilgrims paying homage at the shrines of Christian martyrs and saints whom, they believed, could cure them of their illnesses and afflictions. The shrine of St Thomas Becket at Canterbury raised up to £1,142 annually (PDV £770,000), requiring ten full-time employees to manage the process so that visitors did not disrupt the cathedral's religious services.

Building costs:
- 1234-52 a six bay east end extension at Ely Cathedral cost between £6,000 and £7,000* (PDV £5.2 and £6 million);
- 1245-72 the east end extension, new transepts, five bays of the nave and the chapter house at Westminster Abbey cost £40,000* (£34.2 million);

- 1220-58 Salisbury Cathedral cost a total of £28,000* excluding the west end and spire (£23.9 million);
- 1322-c1340 the octagon tower at Ely Cathedral cost £2,046.35p (£1.63 million);
- 1361-73 the four bay extension to the east end and the Lady Chapel at York Minster cost £6,000* (£4.6 million);
- 1675-1710 total cost of building St Paul's Cathedral in London £736,752 (£101 million);
- 1709-25 cost of building the parish church which later became Birmingham Cathedral cost £5,012 excluding materials and transport (£672,000);
- 1958-62 cost of building Coventry Cathedral was in the region of £985,000 (£24.1 million).

Wages:
- a priest in the 13th Century was paid £3.33p a year* (PDV £2,850);
- in c1300 a labourers weekly rate at Exeter Cathedral ranged from 3p to 5p (£24.75p to £41.25p);
- 1334 William Hurley, the master carpenter responsible for the Ely octagon, was paid £8 a year* (£6,485);
- 1338/9 William of Ramsey, a master mason at Norwich Cathedral was paid £1.05p a year (£836) as a consultant to build the cloisters plus a robe worth 83p* (£661).

Commodities:
- Between the winters of 1266/7 and 1666/7 the cost of a loaf of bread remained unchanged at 0.2p (PDV from £1.71 down to 29p);
- 1410 a master mason's house in York was valued at £30 (£21,615) with goods totalling £180* (£129,700).

Table 1 shows some contemporary costs of building projects, commodities and wages with present day relative values (PDV) added. Those marked with an (*) are from: *Jon Cannon: The Great English Cathedrals and the World that made them 600-1540.*

All the diocese and monastic income was paid into one common fund which was then divided into four, far from equal shares: one went to the bishop or abbot; another to the cathedral or priory chapter; a third to a fabric fund to maintain the buildings and a final one to assist the poor, sick or orphaned. The unequitable nature of this arrangement can be illustrated by the clear discrepancy between the bishop's income and that received by the chapter. In around 1535 just before the Reformation, the annual income received by the Archbishop of Canterbury was £3,233 while the priory got £2,349 (PDV's £1.4 and £1.02 million); Durham bishop received £3,138 and the priory got £1,366

(£1.36 million and £590,000); at Winchester the respective figures were £2,873 and £1,507 (£1.24 million and £651,000); at Ely £2,134 and £1,084 (£922,000 and £468,000); at secular Lincoln the bishop received £2,095 while the chapter got £575 (£905,000 and £248,000) while at York the Archbishop received £2,035 while the cathedral chapter received £747 (£879,000 and £323,000). From these figures it was hardly surprising that one 15th Century Archbishop of York left over £4,000 (£2.7 million) in his will while the Bishop of Ely left a reputed £2,550 (£2.1 million) in 1298.

It was not surprising then that many building projects were funded directly by archbishops and bishops who were by far the wealthiest ecclesiastics in the English medieval church. Thomas of Bayeux, Archbishop of York from 1070-1100, and the bishops of Ripon and Exeter paid the total cost of rebuilding their cathedrals from their own personal wealth while Bishop Northwood of Ely contributed £5,040 (PDV £4.3 million) or just over 75% of the total cost of the east end extension built between 1234-52. William Wykeham paid the complete bill for transforming Winchester Cathedral's nave from Norman to Gothic in 1394 while Richard Poore, who was Bishop of Salisbury, Chichester and Durham, left money to all three in his will and his legacy included the building of the Chapel of Nine Altars at the latter.

The cost of building a cathedral was an enormous undertaking, requiring financing over a long period. The available monies determined the speed, scale and quality of the building with a well-funded building programme being the exception rather than the rule in this era. Whilst it took just 46 years to build Salisbury, York Minster took nearly 250 years to complete. Investigating why this occurred gives a fascinating insight into the problems of cathedral funding in the Middle Ages[5]. As we will see, this fund had to compete with the voracious appetite for money of the Catholic Church in Rome, the English monarch and the Archbishops of York.

Despite the comparative wealth of the York archbishopric, the rebuilding of its Minster started in around 1230 and was not completed until 1472 experiencing frequent and lengthy breaks in building activity. York's enduring dispute with Canterbury over the primacy of the English church began in the 10th Century but got worse and more costly after the Norman Conquest. Indeed it was not uncommon for the two archbishops to have to be physically separated after heated arguments which verged on violence. On one of his frequent canvassing trips to Rome, Walter de Gray (1215-55) is reported to have paid £10,000 (PDV £8.5 million) for his consecration as Archbishop of York. This huge sum diverted money away from the rebuilding of the cathedral which, on his death, had only seen the completion of the south transept and start of the northern one.

Lack of money prevented any further building work during the next four incumbent's terms in office. Godfrey de Ludham (1258-65) saddled his successors with a further £4,000 (£3.4 million) of debt while Walter Gifford's (1266-79) extravagant household expenses totalled £735 (£625,000) in 1268, including £167 (£142,000) on wine alone. Two years later his annual spending rose to £951 (£808,000) and, if the accounts are to be believed, prevented him from giving a single penny to the fabric fund. Archbishop William de Wickwane (1279-85) complained about the continuing payments he had to make to Rome while his successor, Archbishop John Le Romeyn (1286-96), the illegitimate son of a former cathedral treasurer, died destitute after appearing to pay bribes totalling £3,604 (£3 million) to both Rome and the English monarch to overlook this fact. This did not, however, prevent the completion of the chapter house and the commencement of the nave during his time in office. William of Greenfield (1306-16) was threatened with excommunication by the Pope if he did not repay a £4,000 (£3.2 million) loan which forced him to borrow, including a £40 (over £32,000) loan off his valet. Meanwhile work on the new nave stalled.

York had other significant sources of income. It had 36 prebends each equating to about £180 per year (PDV £135,000) which gave a handsome profit after paying a priest only £6 annually (£4,500). Half of all of York's prebends, however, were owned by foreigners. It was hardly surprising that an absent prebend cared little about a cathedral he never visited but the unpopularity of this arrangement erupted when local people discovered that one Italian cardinal passed his money to a Rome hospital when York had its own sick and injured to nurse. Indeed the church critic John Wycliffe claimed that over £100,000 (PDV £75 million) was syphoned out of England in this way – a sum of money that would have built three Salisbury cathedrals.

Another contentious issue was that leading churchmen were appointed by the monarch before being formally rubber-stamped by the Pope. These posts were used as political sweeteners to foster alliances with powerful families, frequently sold for money or given to close family relations. Sometimes these prelate positions were left vacant on purpose so that their incomes went instead to the monarch. This resulted in poorly attended, leaderless chapter meetings which sometimes led to a lack of adequate supervision during major building activities.

William de Melton, Archbishop from 1317-40, made significant loans to kings, barons and bishops as well as being forced to pay for 3,000 civilians in a failed attempt to stave off a Scottish invasion. This reduced his ability to contribute to the building fund although he did donate £400 (PDV £320,000) towards the cost of installing the minster's great west window in 1338/9. When John Thoresby (1352-73) became the Archbishop, the cathedral was in a poor state of repair with a leaking roof. He undertook a vigorous repair programme and commenced work to replace the last major surviving Norman part of the Minster, the east end presbytery. Work commenced in 1361 for which he contributed at least £2,600 (£2 million) of his own money which meant he died in relative poverty.

The three subsequent archbishops added little to the building although the situation was not helped by the fact that three of the deans were Italian and never paid a single visit to York. Work recommenced on the choir in 1388 and was finished by 1410 which included the great east window helped by a £66.56 (PDV £49,900) contribution from King Richard II. In 1407 the central tower collapsed and the cost of its repairs was assisted by Richard Le Scrope (archbishop 1398-1405) in an oblique way. He was executed for his role in a northern uprising against Henry IV, subsequently martyred and his shrine attracted large numbers of pilgrims who made donations including £150 (£110,000) in 1418. Work on the central tower was finally complete and the minster was rededicated in July 1472.

We have seen in this chapter how land and money given by wealthy benefactors in the early Middle Ages was used to rebuild and extend the English cathedral. Later these gifts were utilised for more personal projects in the form of chantry chapels, memorial windows and church furniture frequently branded with family crests and coats-of-arms.

5. PURPOSE
What function did the English Cathedral fulfil?

....

No two English medieval cathedrals are identical: the site, when it was built, the predominant architectural style at the time, the available finance, the patrons' preferences and the designer's interpretation of the project brief all ensured this. Unlike most buildings, their form was not a strict interpretation of the buildings function, namely to provide a suitable space for religious theatre and be built of a quality and size to impress. There was a need to provide both a spiritual and an aesthetic element, to give an appropriate 'atmosphere', be 'aspiring' and 'beautiful.' In addition, churches are full of Christian symbolism: their orientation, shape, height, iconography, proportions, finishes, fixtures and fittings, even their floor levels all have significant religious connotations.

Christians originally used private houses as churches when they were forced to worship in secret but this changed radically when Christianity became the official religion of the Roman Empire in the early 4th Century. Then civic buildings like basilicas were adapted for worship or used as a model with the first purpose-built churches being erected over Rome's catacombs which were the burial grounds of early saints and martyrs outside the city walls. Gradually the cruciform shape was adopted for symbolic reasons, as Christians believed that Jesus Christ was crucified on a similar shaped cross.

All of England's medieval cathedrals are therefore based on the Latin cross (†) with the vertical element usually built on an east / west axis with the shorter eastern arm being the most sacred part of the church housing the High Altar and clergy. The longer western arm or nave is where the congregation are housed, facing to the east, which is usually flanked by shorter-height aisles used for circulation and processions. The west end is the public façade of the church mostly comprising of bell towers and an entrance porch. The horizontal cross beam forms south and north facing transepts whilst a central tower is built over the crossing with high-level windows to admit light into the centre of the church. The tower was frequently topped with a spire, of which only a few survive in this country. From this basic pattern, alterations and additions were undertaken at an amazing frequency as fashion, liturgical rituals, design and new money-making schemes developed. These changes largely affected the east or 'working' end while the transepts and nave underwent far fewer alterations.

All of England's Anglo-Saxon cathedrals were demolished in the first fifty years following the Norman Conquest and were replaced by far grander ones, some so large they could accommodate all of the inhabitants of the adjoining town. The pre-Conquest churches at Glastonbury and Peterborough covered an area of less than 500 square metres, while the Norman ones at York, Lincoln and Winchester were all over $6,000m^2$ with Old St Paul's covering an amazing $8,000m^2$. This contrast in size with the new cathedrals towering over their surrounding landscapes and towns would have clearly demonstrated the power of the new state and its religion over the previous one to the native Anglo-Saxons[6].

The early Norman churches terminated at the east end in a semi-circular apse housing the High Altar and, if they had one, a shrine. The adjacent aisles were finished with a simple square or additional apses as Canterbury and Old Sarum cathedrals. The problem with this dead-end arrangement was the difficulty of accommodating processions and visiting pilgrims who were forced to turn back on themselves. To overcome this problem, Hereford Cathedral brought the High Altar forward by one bay and incorporated an ambulatory behind it which allowed easier access to the apse. A more elaborate alteration was undertaken at Canterbury where the east end was extended by building a semi-circular ambulatory with chapels off whilst retaining the crypt below. This work was started only twenty years after Lanfranc's post-Conquest cathedral was completed and its layout was used as a blueprint for other English monastic cathedrals.

The large amounts of money that shrines dedicated to saints or Christian martyrs generated resulted in every secular and monastic cathedral attempting to acquire some miracle working relic by either applying to Rome to canonise a local worthy or by purchasing body parts like bones, hair or teeth from other religious houses. So desperate were some to get their hands on a relic that they actually resorted to stealing. When Benedict, prior of Canterbury Cathedral, was appointed abbot at Peterborough in 1177, he allegedly removed blood and stained clothing from Thomas Becket's remains to set up a shrine at his new monastery. These relics were originally housed in subterranean crypts sited below the east end but the number of pilgrims overwhelmed this arrangement resulting in shrines and relics being lifted up into the eastern arm of the cathedral and placed behind the High Altar in a feretory.

This resulted in all cathedrals that possessed a shrine having their east ends rebuilt and extended between 1170 and 1220. Canterbury housed Thomas Becket, Chichester St Richard, Durham St Cuthbert, Ely St Ethelreda, Lichfield

St Chad, Lincoln St Hugh, Salisbury St Osmund, Winchester St Swithun, Worcester St Wulfstan and St Oswald, York St William, the majority being former bishops and abbots of the cathedral. We shall see later in chapter eight, that these shrines eventually became richly decorated with precious metals and jewellery and, if they were not adequately protected, were liable to be stolen as happened to St Hugh's at Lincoln in 1364. Pilgrims would enter the cathedral by either the west end or through one of the transepts at a pre-arranged time to be met by a cleric or monk and taken to the shrine where its cover would be lifted by pulleys and ropes to enable the pilgrims to pay homage and make a cash donation.

The need for more chapels for smaller groups and private worship, preferably facing east, was met most frequently by extending the transepts. The most important of these chapels in the Middle Ages was the Lady Chapel, dedicated to the Virgin Mary, the mother of Jesus Christ. From the beginning of the 13th Century all large churches had at least one such chapel, usually sited at the extreme east end but, where this was not possible, it would be placed in or beside a transept as is the case with Ely Cathedral's fine surviving example. Few endured the Reformation but those that did are today used to accommodate the overspill from the main church or host smaller midweek services.

Another important source of church income came from chantry chapels, York Minster for example received 25% of its revenue from them. Wealthy individuals gave money to build, furnish and maintain these in return for the cathedral providing eternal devotion to them and their families. This was an onerous obligation with monks at Durham having to celebrate 7,000 such masses every year while Old St Paul's employed 74 chantry priests to undertake these tasks. At one time there was no less than 36 chantry chapels at York and Lincoln, 30 at Old St Paul's and 24 at Salisbury. Today 42 survive in England's cathedrals: 31 are dedicated to former ecclesiastics, mainly ex-bishops and abbots, eight in memory of wealthy donors while three are for members of the royal family: Henry IV and Edward the Black Prince in Canterbury Cathedral and Prince Arthur, son of Henry VII, in Worcester Cathedral. Of the surviving ones, Winchester has nine, Exeter and Lincoln four each while Canterbury, St Albans and Wells all have three.

Increasingly cathedrals were seen as a good place in which to intern royalty, nobility and the church hierarchy. Originally coffins were buried immediately below the floor with just their lids visible but by the 13th Century these were replaced by grand monuments. Tomb chests with carved stone effigies or bronze figures with highly decorated canopies were erected.

England's cathedrals have a rich heritage of such tombs and monuments devoted to their monarchs: no less than 17 are buried inside Westminster Abbey from Edward the Confessor in 1066 until George II in 1760. King John lies in Worcester, Edward II at Gloucester, William II in Winchester, Henry IV at Canterbury and the recently discovered remains of Richard III in Leicester Cathedral. Memorials to historic English church leaders like Lanfranc, Becket and Theodore can be found inside Canterbury Cathedral.

Ever since the Norman Conquest, the sole focus of worship has been on the raised High Altar located in the east end. The altar was originally used for live sacrifices but today it is used to celebrate the Eucharist where the clergy and congregation share bread and wine symbolising the body and blood of Jesus Christ. The bishop's throne which gives a cathedral its name, is usually adjacent to the choir although the ones at Norwich and Canterbury are sited in the east apse behind the High Altar, its ancient location. The oldest bishop's seat can be found in Exeter Cathedral. It dates from 1312, is made of oak, measures 19 metres in height and cost the princely sum of £6.63 (PDV £5,400) to manufacture. The timber choir stalls face one another and include panelling, canopies and misericords, a tip-up seat with a ledge on the underside which, when raised, would support the elderly and infirm clergy and monks during the long periods of standing. Around 3,500 misericords survive and some are decorated in surprising and explicit detail. As well as the usual Bible stories, they also depicted contemporary society, warts and all: grotesque heads, musical instruments, hunting and even sex scenes. Indeed some were deemed so pornographic that they were removed by the prudish Victorians. If all these functions could not be adequately accommodated in the east end, the actual choir was often moved west of the central crossing into the nave.

The size of the nave enforced the churches sense of awe as well as acting as an important setting for processions and to accommodate a cathedral's numerous altars. The length of the naves in Benedictine monastery cathedrals were particularly impressive with St Albans and Ely each originally having 13 bays while Norwich had 14. Naves were initially not intended for lay-worship except where they doubled up as a parish church, as was the case at St Albans and Peterborough cathedrals. We saw earlier that members of the public were excluded from the east end of cathedrals and abbeys except for taking Holy Communion once a year at Easter or visiting the cathedral's shrine. They played no part in the services being performed, might just about hear what was going on but were prevented from observing them as the presbytery was physically separated from the nave by the pulpitum and, in monastic cathedrals, a rood screen as well. The laity stood in the nave whose floor was covered in straw and mud with only a few stone seats at the bases of columns provided for the old and infirm. It was only after the Reformation that pews were introduced as the practice of lengthy sermons developed.

The pulpitum was typically a solid stone wall built across the nave and continued over the aisles with iron railings and gates to exclude all except clergy and monks from the presbytery. It contained a central opening with a solid door through which the clergy passed, a staircase to a platform above from which sermons and the gospels were preached in the late Middle Ages. A rood is a wooden cross or crucifix which was normally accompanied by figures representing Mary and John who were said to have attended the crucifixion of Jesus Christ. This cross was either suspended from the ceiling by chains above the pulpitum in secular cathedrals or placed on top of an additional timber or stone screen in monastic ones. This partition was known as the rood screen and was typically placed one bay west of the pulpitum. It contained processional doorways on either side through which only monks passed and towards to end of the Middle Ages it also contained a central altar facing the nave from which to preach to the assembled laity.

This strict physical and symbolist division shows the cathedral's ambivalence to the laity. Phrases like 'strangers disturbing the celebrations' or this 'not a parish church' were frequently expressed with members of the public attending being regarded as 'a necessary nuisance.' These barriers were removed following the Reformation but we can see today the problems of trying to hold a communal service where the High Altar is separated from the assembled throng in the nave by the choir, frequently raised and screened off. To overcome this and try for more inclusivity, alternative altars and choirs have been erected in the east end of the nave as has happened for example at Canterbury, Rochester and Norwich cathedrals. It was not surprising that this lack of involvement and contempt shown to the laity frequently led to services being disrupted by noisy, uncouth behaviour in the nave. In 1598, it was reported that religious services were conducted against 'a background of noise and smell caused by children playing and a month's worth of accumulated rubbish' in the nave. This area was often used for a variety of other purposes like hosting miracle plays, as a meeting place for townsfolk as well as for trading and even fighting. Old St Paul's nave provided a short-cut between the north and south sides of the cathedral being used by horses and mules to transport beer, fruit and fish. Its chapels were used as shops selling coal, meat and glassware while its underground vault was let out as a carpenter's workshop.

A central tower was built over the main crossing which, as well as admitting light, acted as a termination for nave, east end and transept roofs. Their construction seems to have tested the medieval master masons technical abilities to the limit as they frequently collapsed: Winchester's in 1107, Ely's in 1322, Lincoln's in 1239 killing three people. Spires were often added onto the tower, built either of timber or stone. Timber was lighter, easier to construct and could be fabricated on the ground before being hoisted into place. Stone spires, usually octagonal shaped, were a more durable solution with permanent scaffolding being retained inside them at the lower level. Lightning was a constant threat, however, causing the demise of Durham's and Old St Paul's in 1429, 1459 and 1561. Gales brought down Norwich's in 1362 and Lincoln's, the tallest one ever constructed, in 1584. Today few survive: Salisbury has England's tallest at 123 metres in height whilst Lichfield has three. West end towers were an important architectural feature, housing the cathedral's bells but, where they were not built, a free standing campanile tower was occasionally provided like the surviving one at Chichester Cathedral. Bells and later clocks were used to assist timekeeping in the locality with the former also being used to announce deaths and warnings of invasions.

The west front was the cathedral's main entrance which tended to be more elaborate and welcoming in secular cathedrals than for monastic ones. These façades were occasionally used as a screen filled with statues, originally colourful and highly decorated. The most spectacular can be seen at Wells which has about 350 sculptured figures probably by Thomas Norreys. Most monastery abbeys were fairly nondescript but Peterborough's magnificent full-height three-arched west front is a notable exception.

Norman architecture's expanse of bare stone walls and small windows offered artists, sculptures and embroiders a perfect blank canvas to enhance the gloomy interior of cathedrals. Churches were a riot of colour, painted in reds, blues and yellows with gold leaf and marble patterned flooring. Wall paintings depicting stories from the Bible were used to teach, caution and entertain the largely illiterate worshippers. Later, colourful stained glass was similarly utilised with the increased size of windows offered by Gothic architecture. Very few original paintings or windows survive as they were whitewashed over or destroyed during the Reformation and the English Civil Wars.

During medieval religious services, which consisted of unaccompanied clerics chanting the Latin psalms, any musical instruments were considered incongruous. The first organs, invented by the ancient Greeks, were used in some Anglo-Saxon churches while a 400-pipe one was employed in the late 10th

Century at Winchester Cathedral which required three players and up to 70 monks to produce the wind. A more sophisticated water-operated pneumatic organ was developed by the Arabs and was introduced into Western Europe by the Normans. These were used to accompany Mass with singing, led by choirs, becoming more common as the Middle Ages progressed. Immediately after the Reformation, however, organs along with all instrumental music, were banned from Protestant worship by the Puritans before being gradually reintroduced when hearty, congregational singing became popular.

6. DESIGN
Who designed the English Cathedral and what was their aspiration?

....

W e should be extremely careful about accepting the notion frequently expressed in the past and often repeated today, that our medieval cathedrals were designed and built by monks or other religious personnel no matter how holy or revered he or she was. Just like present day royal princes, company directors and wealthy clients, they would have been incapable of designing or of physically erecting a sophisticated building like a cathedral unless they had been trained so to do.

We do have some contemporary evidence of monks assisting the hired builders, valuing in some way the spiritual aspect of manual labour. Bishop Hugh of Lincoln is frequently quoted as carrying stones and mortar during 'his' cathedral's construction, possibly as an act of religious penance. Typically, rather less attention was given to the lay master masons who actually designed and supervised its building: Messrs Geoffrey de Noyers, Richard, Michael and Alexander. While it is conceivable that some semi-skilled tasks could have been undertaken by religious clerics, this became much less likely as construction techniques became more complex. Thomas de Northwich, a Benedictine monk at Evesham and described as a 'gifted amateur', was said to be responsible for building the abbey's great tower. Shortly after his death in 1207, however, the tower collapsed although a sympathetic chronicler claimed this was partly due to the misuse of the fabric fund by the abbot[7]. We do know that a few master masons were also members of the clergy and indeed there is evidence that substantial numbers were trained within English and French monasteries from c1000 to c1250. This was not surprising as these institutions had a virtual monopoly on education as well as being a major employer of masons. John Harvey estimates that of the 1,200 architects known in the period from 1050-1500, only about 18 (that is around 1.5%) were certainly or possibly also part of a religious order[8]. This would indicate that it was extremely rare for master masons to become monks or lay-members of a monastery after completing their training.

A typical account from the Middle Ages was the one written by a monk at Ely in 1321[9] describing the collapse of the central tower and how the cathedral's sacrist, Alan de Walsingham "at great labour and expense, had the fallen stone and beams carried out of the church; and as rapidly as possible cleared it of all the dust that had accumulated. And the place where the new tower was to be built he measured out with the skill of an architect into eight divisions, in which eight stone columns supporting the whole edifice should be set up, within which the choir with its stalls should afterwards be built; and he caused it to be dug and searched until he found solid ground on which the foundations of the work could safely be laid. And when these eight places had been strongly consolidated with stones and sand, then at last he began the eight columns with stonework above them; which, in the course of six years, was finished up to the highest string course in the year 1328. And immediately, in that year, the ingenious wooden structure of the new tower, designed with great and astonishing subtlety, to be erected on the said stonework, was begun. And at a very great and heavy cost – especially for the huge beams required for that structure, which had to be sought far and wide, found with much difficulty, bought at a great price, and carried to Ely by land and water, and cut and wrought and cunningly framed for the work by subtle craftsmen, - at last, with God's help, it was brought to an honourable and long-hoped-for finish." This account clearly suggests that the cleric Alan de Walsingham was responsible for constructing one of England's greatest medieval monuments. We saw in chapter three how this misunderstanding might arise and how Walsingham appeared to have no training or experience of design or building. Unlike the monk's report, the cathedral's fabric rolls do disclose the masons or carpenters who undertook the design and supervised the work: John of Ramsey and John Atte Grene were responsible for the stone columns whilst master carpenter William Hurley constructed the timber lantern.

This lack of recognition of both designer and builder whilst giving disproportionate credit to the religious personnel involved with the project was hardly surprising as contemporary chronicles were inevitably written by subservient monks and clerics. The architect, like his fellow painter, sculptor and artisan, tended to remain anonymous in medieval times hidden behind his sponsor, the person who usually took all the credit for the work. This was only to change after the Renaissance period but it has taken until the 20th Century for many of the architects and builders who designed and erected our ancient cathedrals to be identified and given the due credit their work so richly deserves, thanks to research by the likes of John Harvey[10].

We can then be fairly certain that our medieval cathedrals were designed by highly skilled and trained professionals who would invariably be either a master stonemason or, if timber was the dominant material, a master carpenter, the architects of the medieval era. Master Robertus came from Normandy following the Conquest and was employed building St Albans abbey in 1077 because his skill and labour exceeded all other contemporary masons and he was a layman. LF Salzman[11] portrays an architect as an individual who is capable of envisaging a building, complete and in detail before one stone is laid and who is able to convey this vision to the actual builders who turn it into a reality. Indeed the role of a Middle Age master mason was so comprehensive that it would have to embrace up to six other functions found in a modern-day multi-disciplinary construction team encompassing the structural engineer (responsible for designing the sub and super structure), the site engineer (setting out the building on the site), the services engineer (drainage and water supply), quantity surveyor (money and payments), clerk of the works (quality) as well as frequently also being the actual builder or contractor.

Just like a present day architect, a master mason underwent a lengthy training process but, unlike today, it started practically by first having to learn his craft – stonemasonry. Originally, most masons were sons of masons with their skills and knowledge being passed from father to son. Eventually a training system of up to seven years was developed with masons taking on apprentices from around the age of 14. This comprised of four years learning the basic skills of cutting and shaping stone with a further three spent as an 'improver' where they were expected to move away from their master, travelling from job to job to gain experience of different types of work. It was usual at the end of each level that an apprentice would undertake a presentation to his peers to demonstrate his competence which, if successful, was frequently followed by a sumptuous celebration. So by the age of around 21, a mason was fully trained and qualified to work as a 'journeyman', capable of undertaking the essentials of his trade usually for a daily or weekly rate of pay. If a 'journeyman' inherited or married into money, he sometimes opened up his own shop or yard and became an employer, hiring masons, undertaking specific items of work 'at risk' for an inclusive price by signing a binding contract. After a period of time and experience he might then well be considered as a 'master' of his craft by his peers.

Most masons never rose above this 'ordinary' level with very few indeed being capable of designing and supervising a large, complicated building project like a cathedral. The step from 'artisan' to 'designer' mason was a massive one requiring him to possess additional abilities and skills. These were likely to include the capacity to be able to read and write in French, Latin and eventually English; to be able to communicate unambiguously to both wealthy patrons and the various building trade operatives; to be proficient at sketching freehand and of drawing full-size or to scale using mechanical aids like the compass, the square and the straight-edge; and most importantly he needed to know the rules and techniques of design involving geometry and proportion.

These specialist skills would be learned from royal projects, cathedral and monastery schools, his travels but mainly from his fellow master masons.

The five Orders of Architecture date from the ancient Greeks who laid down rules governing the proportions of buildings, their apertures, columns and beams. These were written down by the Roman architect Vitruvius in the 1st Century BC and formed the basis of all medieval design affecting a buildings plan, section, elevation and even its detailing. The Greek mathematician Euclid's textbook *'The Elements'* became widely available in Western Europe in around 1120 and his rules of geometry are still taught today. The three most employed rectangles, whose vertical and horizontal sides have ratios of 1:√2 or 1.414, 1:1.618 the so called golden section or cut and 1:√3 or 1.732, based on the 60^0 equilateral triangle, could all be established using geometry and drawn by straight edge and compass.

The majority of masonic rules, however, were unwritten, strictly controlled, only being passed between master masons by word of mouth usually in the security of the masons' lodge. Indeed academics and mathematicians have spent years studying Middle Age cathedrals to try to establish their design secrets without much success. Secrecy was a feature of the stonemason's craft in which breaches could result, in the most extreme cases, in death. In 1099, when the son of master mason Plebeus told the Bishop of Utrecht (Netherlands) how the churches basement would be made watertight, his father took the most extreme action and murdered the bishop to preserve the secret[12]. These ancient masonic ideas and rules today form the basis of the worldwide freemasonry movement which dates from the late 18th Century.

After successfully completing his apprenticeship a mason would be given a 'mark' which he could use as a signature on completed work. These marks, which were commonly used from around 1200, can be found extensively in English and continental cathedrals and have reached almost mythical status. Three theories have been put forward for their use: they were to identify works carried out by individuals working on piecework for the benefit of the paymaster; they were used by masons to sign off work undertaken by other masons working for them as being up to an acceptable standard or they were used as an advert to publicise their work.

Medieval architects appear undaunted in copying their fellow masons' work. It has often been cited of the similarities between Edward the Confessor's Westminster Abbey church and the ones at Bernay and Jumièges, whilst its successor had a likeness to Reims and Amiens cathedrals. Distinct regional patterns developed with the west front of Exeter resembling that at Wells in south-west England. The latest techniques, trends and architectural styles were keenly sought and followed whilst increased mathematical knowledge of structures and forces led to more precisely cut masonry and thinner mortar joints. This in turn resulted in more slender walls and piers with increased roof and ceiling vaulting spans. Despite these trends, progress was predominantly through trial and error with master masons being keenly competitive, constantly experimenting and stretching their knowledge to the limit. This empiric approach resulted in frequent and spectacular building failures particularly in the difficult elements of ceiling vaulting, taller towers and foundation works.

A cathedral's design would start with the floor plan based on a series of squares or the three favoured proportional rectangles which would be repeated until the required size of the church was achieved. From the plan, elevations and sections were generated again based on proportions with a repeated vertical bay arrangement. This was often in the form of three horizontal sections: arcade, triforium and clerestory with the main piers and arches emphasising the verticality of the design. Large areas of masonry were broken down by Gothic designers using plinths, string courses, panelling, wall/head decoration, parapets and blind arcading before artists and sculptures added colour and imagery.

Two distinct types of drawing were required to convey the architect's ideas to the patron and to the building operatives. In the first, freehand sketches including a ground floor plan plus elevations, were required frequently accompanied by a 3D model to assist a layperson to better understand the proposition. A 17th Century model of the third of Christopher Wren's five proposals for the rebuilding of St Paul's survives and can be viewed in the cathedral. Constructed of oak and plaster in 1673 it is six metres in length and cost £600 (PDV £87,000), the equivalent price for a contemporary house. The second type, known as 'working' or production drawings, were the ones from which the cathedral was actually built. These would be large scale, some being full sized, showing plans, sections, elevations and details of the various important elements - columns, window tracery and ceiling vaults. From these drawings, templates made from oak, iron plate or lead would be produced and delivered to the working masons who would replicate them onto the stones for shaping. Before the use of paper in the early 16th Century, these drawings were done on wood, cloth, plaster or expensive parchment, which could be cleaned and re-used. It is therefore not surprising that no working drawings of cathedrals survive in this country although many have in Europe.

In order to discharge his responsibilities on a large building project, the master mason would require two distinct areas in which to work. The mason's lodge at its most simplistic would be no more than a covered shed but, when attached to cathedrals where there was continuous maintenance and minor works, was likely to be a permanent feature. When a large building project was in progress it became a far larger multi-purpose facility likely to be the equivalent to today's site office being used for meetings and discussing the project. It would also act as a workshop where stone was cut and shaped on workbenches as well as having drawing equipment, dining, resting and sleeping facilities. Each lodge had its own set of rules overseen by the master covering issues like the length of the working day, times of meal breaks and penalties for breaking the regulations. For smaller drawings, trestle tables and 'T' squares were used but larger scale ones, often drawn full-sized, were done on timber sheets or, more commonly, on plaster floors in a tracing room, the present day architects' drawing office. These floors were plastered over and reused with two surviving at York and Wells cathedrals. Unlike all other building trades at this time which were organised as locally-based craft guilds, stonemasons were required to travel nationwide to undertake their profession. These mason lodges were therefore an important feature in their training, education and for exchanging knowledge as well as providing accommodation and hospitality.

After completing the drawings, master masons supervised the building works whilst frequently doing some of the more intricate stonework themselves. Increasingly they were contracted to undertake whole elements of the building work, being responsible for purchasing the materials and for hiring the workmen. So as early as 1261, Nicholas de Biard, a Dominican preacher, was complaining that master masons were directing the works by word of mouth alone, seldom or never dirtying their hands and yet receiving far more money than others. He describes them "carrying a yard stick and with gloves on their hands, saying to others 'cut it for me this way[13]", a criticism of the professional architect that can still be heard today.

It was not surprising that master masons who held more responsible positions requiring greater skills, commanded higher salaries, enjoying greater job security with more 'perks.' It was not uncommon for them to receive twice that of an 'ordinary' mason and up to four times the amount if they were particularly renowned. Their contracts might be for several years, even for life and include a pension with sick pay. Their remuneration package often also included food, clothing, aprons, gloves and even shoes. In 1359/60 Ely Cathedral employed John Stubbard at a rate of £5.20p (PDV £3,980) per year plus a robe. A master mason, hired by Durham Cathedral in 1398, was given a cloth gown every year, a daily loaf of white bread, a gallon of ale and meat in addition to his annual fee. The same cathedral engaged master mason John Bell in 1488 paying him £7.16 (£4,830) a year for life but requiring him to train an apprentice every ten years.

Originally, the medieval architect would live near to the site, controlling the project on a full-time basis. In 1359 at Hereford Cathedral, John of Evesham signed a contract requiring him to live in Hereford, to work diligently on the fabric, to teach others under him and not to work elsewhere without getting permission. For this he was given a house for which he paid rent of 50p per year (PDV £385), a daily loaf of bread and 15p a week (£115) for life. If he fell ill for one or two weeks he would continue to be paid, anything longer his pay would be reduced to 5p per week (£38). Later the master mason became more of a supervising visitor, probably indicating that they were responsible for more than one project at a time, appointing an assistant or clerk of the works to deal with more day-to-day matters. In 1337 William of Ramsey was employed by Lichfield Cathedral chapter to construct the presbytery for which he was paid £1.10 (£880) for each eight-day visit plus 33p (£264) for travel expenses for himself and his team.

John Harvey[14] gives a fascinating insight into the working life of a 14th Century master mason. Thomas Witney was born in the Oxfordshire town after which he was named in around 1270. He worked on St Stephen's chapel in the Palace of Westminster, London for a year in 1292/3 and, after a nine month break, again from July until September 1294. His wages of 14p a week (PDV £116) would indicate he was a fully trained but junior stonemason. After an interlude, he re-appeared in around 1315 in charge of building Winchester Cathedral's presbytery. From 1316 until about 1342 he was also master mason at Exeter Cathedral responsible for finishing the main crossing, constructing the nave and west front. He built the pulpitum, reredos, sedilia and the timber bishop's seat which would indicate he was proficient in both stone and timber, being paid 15p per week (PDV £121) and a further 25p (£202) bonus on his departure from his rented house in the cathedral's close in 1324. It is believed he was also employed as the master mason at Wells Cathedral building the Lady Chapel, the retro-choir and central tower which has details similar to his work at Exeter. The nave windows at Malmesbury Abbey (Wiltshire) and the central crossing at Merton College, Oxford dating from 1330-2 also have comparable features. He died in around 1340 in his early seventies and his son, J. de Sparkeforde, also became a master mason.

Henry Yeveley was the best known master mason of the Middle Ages thanks mainly to a book written about him by John Harvey[15]. In 1356 he was a hewer mason helping to formulate the London masons' regulations and was promoted to work on royal projects from around 1360, where he eventually became master mason until his death aged 80 in 1399. He was known as a 'devisor of masonry' at Westminster Abbey in 1369 being paid 5p a day (PDV £38). Yeveley undertook many other projects and roles including working as a building contractor, supplying materials, designing and working on London's Guildhall, Westminster Hall, Canterbury Castle and royal memorials. These brought him considerable wealth enabling him to own extensive properties which included three country manors, two shops, his main house in London as well as land in Essex.

In the 17th Century, a completely different kind of architect emerged in England. He was not a trained artisan but was a well-travelled academic named Inigo Jones (1573-1652). Although there is some evidence that he served as an apprentice joiner at one time, he made his name as a designer of theatre scenery and costumes for which he produced beautiful and detailed drawings. He was 37 years old before he turned his attention to architecture, travelling extensively around Italy, sketching buildings and studying Vitruvius. On his return to this country he undertook a series of building commissions, eventually being appointed surveyor-general of the king's works in 1615. This set a trend for he was succeeded in 1660 first by Sir John Denham, a poet, and then by Sir Christopher Wren (1632-1723). Wren studied Latin and physics at Oxford University before becoming involved in astronomy, mathematics and physics prior to taking up architecture. Despite not training either as a craftsman or an architect, his design to replace the burnt out and derelict St Paul's Cathedral was eventually accepted. Amazingly Wren was also credited with designing and building no less than 52 other City of London churches destroyed by the Great Fire, an unrivalled achievement although his assistant master masons, Joshua Marshall and Edward Strong, are almost universally overlooked.

Finally we have an example of how competition between patrons influenced the design and building of a cathedral. The City of Liverpool expanded enormously with the opening of the docks in the 18th Century, attracting both Protestants and Catholics particularly from Scotland and Ireland. After Roman Catholic emancipation in 1850, three attempts were made to build a cathedral for the faith over the following one hundred years. Only the Lady Chapel was completed on the first proposal before money ran out forcing Edward Pugin to abandon his massive proposal to build a cathedral in Everton in 1856. An even more ambitious scheme by Sir Edwin Lutyens which would have created the second largest church in the World, started on a different site in 1933 which was to be longer with an even larger dome than St Peter's in Rome. Again spiralling costs estimated at a staggering £27 million (PDV £1,194 million) in 1941, meant that only the crypt was completed by 1958. The current Catholic cathedral, consecrated in 1967, stands above this crypt, being built in an untraditional circular shape in only five years under architect Frederick Gibberd. These proposals appear to have spurred the Anglicans to build a comparable cathedral for themselves. Commenced in 1903, two World Wars prevented it from being fully completed until 1978, during which the original design and even some completed works were revised and rebuilt with its designer Giles Gilbert Scott dying 18 years before it was finished. This gigantic structure is the world's longest cathedral (St Peter's in Rome and the modern one in Africa's Ivory Coast are both called 'basilicas') and is currently the world's seventh largest church. It is interesting to speculate that the reason for this cathedral's size was the direct result of competition caused by Liverpool's sectarian divide.

7. THE BUILDING
How was the English Cathedral built and by whom?

T he logistics of undertaking a large scale construction project in the Middle Ages was a daunting proposition with the number of workers required to build it likely to far exceed the population of the adjoining city. 95% of England's populace at the time lived in rural settlements with most towns having only a few hundred residents. Some like Norwich, Lincoln, Winchester and York had somewhere between five and six thousand while the largest, London, had approximately 50,000 citizens. So ignoring women and children, the available local labour was likely to be only a third of these figures. When Beaumaris Castle in north Wales was built in the late 13th Century some 1,800 operatives were employed including 400 stonemasons, 30 smiths and carpenters assisted by over 1,000 labourers. 30 boats and over 160 wagons and carts were used to transport the materials to site. Cathedral building would require similar numbers but with an even higher percentage of skilled and semi-skilled operatives.

These workers would arrive from all over England and often Europe. A large building project in 1362 at Windsor hired 29 masons from Yorkshire with others coming from as far afield as Lincolnshire, Lancashire, Shropshire, Hereford, Nottingham and Derby. All required accommodation, food, workshops, toilets, meeting and resting facilities which necessitated the building of a large number of temporary timber buildings equating to a largish town. Materials had to be purchased, transported and stored while items like tools, carts, mortar and paint had to be manufactured or mixed on site in an era way before they could be purchased ready-made off the shelf. Several cathedral cities eventually became a catalyst for large numbers of specialist skilled building trades: goldsmiths, blacksmiths, sculptors, joiners and glazers.

England was fortunate in that it possessed plenty of natural resources which eventually reduced the need to import materials for building and cut the enormous cost of transport. Suitable stone was discovered throughout the country; timber was abundant; clay, lead and tin were mined; bricks and flint were used whilst iron could be forged on site. Failing all else, old buildings could simply be plundered as was the case in the building of St Albans Cathedral where the adjoining Roman settlement of Verulamium was looted for its materials.

There were two main ways of organising building works in this era. Initially the direct labour method was used whereby the cathedral's appointed administrator, the 'keeper of the fabric', was in charge of hiring the required labour as well as purchasing and transporting the materials to site. He was assisted in this by the 'master of the works', usually a lay master stonemason, who dealt with design and technical matters as well as supervising the building work. This method put far too much responsibility onto the patron so a second procurement system developed in which specific elements of work were contracted for an agreed 'lump sum' price which would include both labour and materials. An example of this occurred in 1388 when master mason Henry Yeveley was contracted to build a new façade for the south transept of Old St Paul's Cathedral for an agreed fixed sum of £300 (PDV £228,000). Some elements of this lump sum work would be further sub-contracted to specialist tradesmen with written contracts gradually being introduced stipulating in detail the work to be undertaken, the price to be paid and the time in which to do it, more or less as we know it today.

The building of Salisbury Cathedral in the 13th Century was unusual in that it was erected on a virgin or 'greenfield' site as the vast majority of England's cathedrals were built on the sites of former ones. Geographically imposing locations were particularly sought after but where this was not possible, like in flat landscapes, then the buildings themselves would frequently incorporate a feature to improve this sense of domination with the use of spires, towers, size or imposing facades. Sites needed to be big enough, reasonably level and accessible for visitors, materials and provisions both during their construction and after occupation. A good supply of firewood for fuel and running water for drinking, cooking, ablutions and transport were essential which is why most cathedrals are located near to rivers or their tributaries.

Once the patron had approved the design, the budget and the programme the construction phase of the operation could commence. Amazingly part of this process is even described in a William Shakespeare play![16] The site would first need to be 'set up' which would involve finding and employing key personnel; protecting any structures to be retained with the remainder having to be demolished; the working area levelled and erecting the extensive site accommodation.

We noted earlier that it was common practice for churches to be orientated on an east-west axis although St Peter's Basilica in Rome and Liverpool's Anglican Cathedral were both built north-south because of site constraints. Some believe the easterly direction is because of the desire to face the Holy Land, which is actually south-east of England, or towards where it was thought that paradise is located. In fact the most likely reason was to replicate the ancient pagan ritual of facing the direction of the sun at first light, which obviously changes throughout the year. On the summer solstice, when the longest hours of daylight occurs in the northern hemisphere on 21 June, the sun rises in a due north-east direction (45°); at the spring and autumn equinoxes on 22 March and 22 September, the sun rises due east (90°) whilst on the winter solstice when the shortest hours of daylight happens on 21 December, the sun rises due south-east (135°). Nominal east was therefore established at each site by observing when the rising sun first appeared on the cathedral's patron's saint day. It is for this reason that all of England's medieval cathedrals have slightly different orientations. Whilst most are +/- 5° of 90° (due east), Lichfield at 55° is the most north-east facing and Rochester at 129° the most south-east orientated which gives us a clue when each celebrated their original patron's saint day.

Once the cathedral's bearings had been ascertained, the master mason would set out the building on the ground using, as the abbot of Ramsey Abbey observed at the turn of the first Millennium, "the straight line of the rule, the threefold triangle and the compasses." All traditional units of measurement were based on the human body and varied from place to place with the foot (from 296mm to 335mm, now 304.8mm) and the cubit (at just over 450mm being the length from the elbow to tip of middle finger) being commonly used. Gridlines would be set out at either 8, 16 or 32 cubit squares, using 3:4:5 triangulation to ascertain right angles (90°) and 8 cubit long iron rods or perches (about 3.6 metres). Pegs and cord were employed to mark the location of the foundations, which would be excavated until suitable stable, load-bearing ground was found. At York this was over seven metres in depth whilst at Salisbury it was a mere 1.2 metres deep. Where this proved difficult, in say the marshy areas of East Anglia, timber piles were hammered into the ground by dropping a heavy block of stone onto the head of the wooden uprights. If the underground remains of a former church could not be removed, the new sub-structure was simply moved to avoid it. The excavations were filled up to ground level with compacted stone, rubble and mortar.

The first stone blocks were laid onto the foundations with great ceremony with a contemporary account[17] of this process surviving from Salisbury Cathedral in 1220: "On the day of St Viral the martyr, which was 28 April, was laid the foundation of the new church of Salisbury..... The bishop himself laid the first stone on behalf of Pope Honorius, who had given leave for the removal of the church of Salisbury; the second he laid on behalf of Stephen, Archbishop of Canterbury and Cardinal of the Holy Roman Church, who was at that time engaged with the king on the Welsh border; the third he added to the fabric on his own behalf; the fourth stone was laid by William Longsword, Earl of

Salisbury while the fifth was by Ela de Viteri, Countess of Salisbury, wife of the said Earl, a woman worthy of praise as being full of the fear of God."

Work on building the cathedral's masonry walls would start at its more important east end and then progress westwards to include transepts, the central crossing and, for structural stability, a bay or so of the nave. Lack of funds frequently delayed the completion of the nave and west front with Old St Paul's taking over a century to complete whilst Westminster Abbey's was not finished for more than 150 years. The massive increase in stone buildings required for the Norman kings, his military and the state religion, necessitated a simultaneous increase in the number of stonemasons with, not surprisingly, demand frequently outstripping supply. When this occurred, royal projects were given priority because they were able to force or press gang masons to work on them. 145 were impressed to labour on Westminster Abbey in 1292, with each English county being given a quota of masons they had to provide. Local sheriffs were given authority to imprison those who refused to go or those that subsequently absconded.

The most skilled stonemasons were the 'freemasons' who carved, shaped and finished the blocks of stone. They worked on the facing work as well as on ornamental screens, sculptural figures, column capitals and intricate architectural details. The stone walls we see in cathedrals are not solid stone; they are in fact two faced stone walls with the cavity between them filled with rough rubble and mortar. The stone was first loosely reduced in size with an axe before being finely dressed with chisels. In this, freemasons were assisted by 'rough masons', 'layers' or 'setters' and 'hard-hewers' who physically laid the stones in place, roughly reduced them when received from the quarry and undertook all the foundation, infill and hidden masonry works. Labourers were responsible for transporting the materials to where they were required while the mortarmen mixed the lime, sand and water needed for bedding and jointing the stone.

Obtaining an adequate and economic supply of the vast quantities of quality stone required for the building of a cathedral was a major consideration and, until its discovery in this country, had to be imported in huge quantities from Normandy. Transportation costs were a significant factor and it has been estimated that the price of transportation equalled the cost of the stone at a distance of only 12 miles. Norwich Cathedral was largely built of stone imported from Caen for which the transport costs were nearly three times the price of the material. This included a freight ship from France to Yarmouth, unloading it onto barges to Norwich and finally getting it from the wharf to the site.

Limestone was eventually found widely throughout England from Yorkshire to Dorset whilst other less suitable stone like chalk, Kentish ragstone and flint was used in the cores of walls before being faced with limestone ashlar. If suitable stone was available, the cathedral chapter had three options: they could buy the quarry outright and run it as a commercial venture; they could hire the quarry for a period of time or else purchase the stone from privately owned ones. If a cathedral possessed its own quarry where substantial deposits were found, it brought them considerable wealth. Peterborough's monastery owned the nearby Barnack quarry which not only provided the sandy limestone from which they built their abbey but they also managed to sell the surplus stone to nearby Ely to erect parts of their cathedral. Extracting the stone from the quarry was a physically demanding task with picks, axes, levers and wedges being used before the blocks were reduced by splitting and sawing. One way of reducing transportation costs was to cut the stone at the quarry to the required size but this necessitated the designs and templates to be finalised earlier in the process as opposed to undertaking this work later on site. Only comparatively light loads could be transported by horse, ox and cart due to the poor state of contemporary roads. For heavier and bulkier items water transport was the preferred option with boats, barges and their crew being either bought outright or hired for the purpose. England's extensive navigable rivers and streams were utilised with small stretches of temporary canals often being dug to the actual cathedral site.

Once the walls had reached 1.2m in height, it was necessary to provide scaffolding which gave the stonemasons a raised working platform from which to work. Tall timber uprights, horizontal poles (putlogs) and diagonal members to provide stability were lashed together with ropes and willow branches. Whole trees were frequently used – for the vertical members at Exeter Cathedral 15 great poplar and 100 alder trees were purchased for the nave scaffolding in 1324 at a cost of 58p (PDV £470). Each scaffolding lift (level) was accessed by wooden ladders or inclined hurdles. In the early Middle Ages, materials were stored on the scaffolding which necessitated substantial members resting on the ground with the horizontal sections built into the masonry. Later, with the development of more sophisticated lifting devices materials could be stored on the ground which meant that scaffolding became lighter and was able to be bracketed off the masonry with permanent staircases incorporated in the cathedral to provide vertical access.

The lateral forces from ceiling vaults and roofs onto the masonry was counteracted by thickening the wall, known as buttresses. These thrusts were eventually opposed by 'flying' or free standing buttresses which, along with increasing the downward weight by the use of pinnacles, became a major feature of Gothic architecture. Timber templates, the size of window and door openings, were built into the masonry walls as work progressed. These supported the masonry arch above which was divided into segments of individual stones or voussoirs with the all-important keystone at its centre. The timber support would be kept in place until the mortar between the voussoirs had set, before being moved onto the next opening. Gothic architecture allowed for windows to be greatly increased in size but the restricted dimensions of glass meant that apertures had to be broken down by intricate masonry tracery and lead glazing bars. These large windows were drawn full-size on the tracing room floor and became an important feature of English cathedrals, the most impressive being the ones at Gloucester Cathedral and York Minster.

Unlike earlier civilisations, the Middle Age builders did not have the advantage of employing large numbers of unpaid enslaved labour to undertake the manual labouring tasks. Smaller items could be physically moved up the building by hand using hods and stretchers but the bulkier and heavier items like stone and timber had to be raised by a variety of lifting devices. The most common of these was the windlass, a circular drum in which operatives either walked in like a treadmill or else pushed down the projecting timber staves by hand. It has been estimated that an average sized man could lift nearly one and a half tons in weight with an efficient windlass. The smaller devices would be moved as building work progressed but the larger ones were built into the cathedral's structure with at least three surviving today. Durham has one built into its north-west tower dating from around 1220. Peterborough has a complete one with oak staves which could either be stood on like a rotary ladder or pushed down by hand. The windlass in Salisbury's spire probably dates from when the cathedral was built in the 13th Century but was reassembled in 1762. Ropes would be wound around the spindles of these machines, attached to baskets, barrels or other receptacles into which the materials to be lifted would be placed. Larger items would require the use of slings, masonry grips or scissors.

As most medieval buildings were built of timber, so carpenters and joiners were the most commonly employed building operatives in this country. As well as being responsible for the cathedral's roof, fixtures and fittings, they also undertook numerous other tasks like constructing carts and barrows, scaffolding, hoisting devices, the temporary centring for stone arches and vaults, templates for stone designs as well as being responsible for providing the vast amount of temporary buildings required for a large scale construction project.

Getting enough quality timber was another major obstacle to overcome. The ancient forests of England were predominately owned by the king and his barons but abbots and bishops also held a substantial number. Oak was by far and away the most popular building timber which grew plentifully in most areas of the country and, where it did not, could be fairly easily transported by water. It has been estimated that Norwich Cathedral alone contains timber from over 680 oak trees whilst William I's forest at Hempage was decimated by a gang of carpenters who spent four days and nights stripping it bare for timber to rebuild Winchester Cathedral. Individual trees were selected by the patron and master carpenter for large structural elements like beams and joists. For the octagon at Ely in 1322, which required an estimated 450 tons of timber, the sacrist Alan of Walsingham accompanied John the Carpenter to Chicksands in Bedfordshire and spent £9 (PDV £7,300) on buying 20 oak trees. Other varieties of English timber like beech, elm, poplar, willow, ash and chestnut were used but all had significant disadvantages, tending to warp and be of poorer quality. As well as structural timber, oak was also used for partitions and boarding which was placed on roof trusses to support the roof covering. From the late 13th Century, fir and deal started to be imported for these purposes from the Baltic States via the North Sea to east coast ports stretching from Dover to Newcastle.

There was two types of timber roofs used in cathedrals. In the older version, decorated timber would be placed directly onto the underside of the roof trusses so the roof's shape could still be ascertained from below. These were easier and cheaper to construct, less weighty but were more susceptible to fire. A later more commonly seen closed roof was employed by which the roof was hidden from view by a lower level masonry ceiling vaulting. Both types can be seen at Peterborough Cathedral which has the country's only surviving original painted timber ceiling in its nave as well as an early 16th Century fan-vaulted stone ceiling in the retro-choir extension.

Lead mining in England has an ancient history with plumbers not only using the material for roof covering but also for rainwater downpipes, gutters and ornate gargoyles. It replaced thatch and timber shingles as the preferred roof finish for cathedrals, being more durable, capable of being re-used and less susceptible to fire once it had been laid. It was, however, very expensive and therefore was susceptible to being stolen. In 1222, 20 tons of lead for Winchester cost £27.30 (PDV £23,340) with carriage costing a further £1.60

(£1,370) while in 1474, over £187 (£126,000) was spent covering three bays of the nave roof at Westminster Abbey. Most lead in this period came from Derbyshire but was traded from the coastal port of Boston in Lincolnshire, from where it was transported throughout the country by river and sea.

Glass was first used in this country in late Anglo-Saxon churches, before which wooden shutters or oiled linen was employed to cover window openings. This white glass was obtained from south-east England and the Midlands which could then be painted and re-fired which would fuse the paint to the glass. After the Conquest, better quality coloured glass was imported from Normandy and other parts of France, being produced by adding metallic oxides like cobalt (for blue), copper (green), iron (red) and manganese (purple). This process was eventually replicated in England, largely centred round cathedral cities. Glaziers first cracked the glass to a rough size with heated iron tools before the final shaping was done by rubbing away the glass edges with nippers. Diamond cutters were not used until the 17th Century.

Internally, Purbeck and Corfe marble was widely employed in almost all cathedrals in the period from 1170 to 1350. As well as being used for flooring in the east end, it was also utilised for fittings, finishes and statues before eventually being superseded by plaster of Paris, alabaster or gypsum. From the 13th Century, ceramic raised or sunken relief floor tiles became popular with highly complex patterns incorporating coloured stones and marble. These tiles were manufactured in areas like Wiltshire, Derbyshire and Cheshire.

With the building nearing completion, fixtures and fittings were designed and installed. Wood or stone screens divided up the church and chapels, both physically and symbolically. Items like the bishop's throne, choir stalls including sedilia seats for the clergy were made by the joiners and decorated iron gates and railings by the metal smiths. The High Altar was initially a simple table but, as it was the focal point of the service, it became more elaborate, incorporating a canopy with a reredos screen behind. Finally the cathedral would be decorated. Walls and ceilings were white washed before artists undertook paintings and free-standing sculptures of religious figures, kings, spirits, demons and symbolic foliage would be placed around the cathedral and in wall niches.

The medieval building season stretched from March to the end of October. Laying stone in sub-zero temperatures affected the mortar so could not be undertaken in winter with partly completed walls having to be protected from frost by straw and thatch. Cathedrals tended to keep specialist tradesmen employed over the winter in covered, heated lodges or workshops to prepare complicated carved items of masonry or prefabricated timber fixtures and fittings. These elements would then be installed during the following building season. The detailed records of the rebuilding of Westminster Abbey from April until December 1253 show that while the total workforce in the summer varied between 216 and 433 and was split 50/50 between skilled and unskilled, in the winter just 100 were retained split 70/30 in favour of the skilled operative.

The first attempt to regulate wages came in 13th Century London with carpenters, masons and tilers being paid 1.25p per day (PDV £10.69) with food, 1.67p (£14.28) without it. Freemasons would get slightly more than this, plasterers slightly less with labourers and assistants earning from between 0.63p and 1.05p (£5.39 and £8.98) per day. In 1327, the chief mason at York was paid 2.5p a day (£21.38) while at the same time Exeter Cathedral's five basic wage rates ranged from 8.33p to 11.25p (£71.22 to £96.19) per week in summer, 7.3p to 9.38p (£62.42 to £80.20) in winter. These rates would remain constant until they rose following the labour shortage caused by the Black Death later in the century. Women played only a small part in medieval building operations and was usually confined to unskilled or casual work. At Durham in 1532, women were employed to carry mud to make walls being paid 1p a day (PDV £4.32) whilst a year later eight women were transporting stone for 1.5p a day (£6.48). In contrast, women were employed at Ripon Cathedral being paid the same rate as men.

The length of day was dependant on the available daylight, typically 8.75 hours in winter and up to 12.25 hours in summer when hours of work ran from 5am to 7.45pm and included 30 minute breaks for breakfast, 90 for dinner and a siesta and 30 for an afternoon drink. In winter; one hour was allowed for dinner and 15 minutes for an afternoon drink while work on a Saturday usually finished earlier than a weekday. Christmas and Easter holidays usually extended from four days to a week while saint, feast and anniversary days could total up to 27 days a year, with workers not always being paid for these.

We saw in chapter four how the progress of cathedral building was dependent on adequate cashflow, with works frequently suspended until more funds were forthcoming. Monk Gervase of Canterbury gives the most detailed, contemporary account of building work at Canterbury Cathedral undertaken for a decade from 1174[18]. At 9 o'clock on 5th September 1174 fire broke out outside the monastery walls destroying three cottages. A strong southerly wind blew cinders and sparks onto the adjoining cathedral roof dropping between the lead joints into the roof space setting alight the beams which were hidden above the ceiling. Everyone went home unaware of this but the fire eventually burst through the roof and the alarm was raised. The monks fought the fire but were driven back by half burnt roof timbers which fell into the presbytery setting fire to the wooden seats, scorching the walls and damaging the columns up to ten metres from the ground. The roof was completely destroyed, leaving it open to the elements. The undamaged nave was used for services for over five years with the monks only separated from the laity by a low wall. Opinion differed between the English and French specialists consulted on whether to repair the east end or demolish it completely and rebuild. Eventually William of Sens, a specialist in both stone and timber, undertook a detailed survey and concluded that the structure was unsafe and needed to be demolished completely and rebuilt east of the bell tower. After lengthy debate, the monks eventually agreed with this conclusion and William was commissioned to undertake the works. He procured stone from Normandy, giving profiles to his masons for shaping the stone. The east end was demolished and the first four columns erected before the winter of 1175. The work continued until the spring of 1178 when William fell some 17 metres when a timber beam and masonry collapsed. Severely bruised he was confined to bed and instructed an 'industrious and ingenious' monk on how the works should proceed. It was noted that this appointment caused much 'malice and envy' from the higher ranked masons whom he instructed. William was unable to continue his work and returned home to France in the winter of 1178 being replaced by a mason known as William the Englishman. The monks eventually returned to their sanctuary on 19th April 1180 and, after the works were suspended in 1183 due to lack of funds, they were not fully completed until 1184.

The problems encountered between the building occupier and their contractor is not a modern day phenomenon although hopefully not as serious as the quarrel that occurred at Westminster Abbey in August 1324 between seven masons and seven monks that resulted in one of the masons being murdered. Likewise construction problems, fraudulent practices and poor quality workmanship go back centuries. A report by the Master of the Works has been preserved in the York Minster Fabric Rolls relating to work being carried out on the cathedral in January 1345. The chronicler gives a litany of problems: masons being overpaid, paid when absent or had undertaken no work; timber, stone and lime stolen from site; one carpenter being unable to work at heights due to his old age; the master mason's instructions were ignored with cranes being described as being rotten and worthless. Chester's Lady Chapel was built 1265-90 and Lincoln's cloisters between 1296 and 1310, both soon failed after completion and it was discovered they had been built without foundations. In 1460 the unsafe nature of Ripon Cathedral's tower was said to have been caused by the carelessness, neglect and ignorance of the craftsmen. As LF Salzman[19] sagely notes "if the British workman of the present day is not as good as he used to be, he probably never was."

8. POST COMPLETION
How and why has the English Cathedral changed since it was completed?

The interior of a present day English cathedral is a bare replica of how it originally looked being stripped of its colour, imagery and most of its furnishings. What remains of its medieval fixtures and fittings have been dwarfed by later Victorian and modern alterations and additions. The inside of a Middle Age cathedral was full of statues and monumental effigies, walls and windows were bright with painting, altars had images in gold and silver. Everywhere there were bronzes and alabasters, enamels and ivories, precious stones and jewellery, illustrated service books, colourful needlework and embroidery displays. This chapter will look at why these changes occurred since our medieval cathedrals were largely completed in the 16th Century.

Throughout Europe during the Middle Ages, it was widely believed that a good monk should be a poor monk and, when this was no longer the case, that monasteries considerable wealth should be confiscated and put to better use for education, social welfare or to support parish churches with their pastoral work. Many within English society concluded that monasteries were irrelevant, an anachronism from a by-gone age and had been corrupted by centuries of excessive wealth and power. Followers of the new Protestant faith thought that the Catholic Church had moved too far away from the original teachings of the Bible, putting unnecessary divisions between the clergy and laity, using obscure Latin rather than plain English. They also believed they were corrupted by indulgencies and bribes, gave too much reverence to the Virgin Mary and worshipped obscure saints and their relics, all of which they regarded as 'craven images.'

The precedent for closing monasteries and re-distributing their wealth was set in 1524 when the Pope gave King Henry VIII permission to close St Frideswide's at Oxford and convert it into an education college, initially Cardinal later Christ Church College, which today houses the city's cathedral. The proceeds of the monastery's land and manors were used to endow the college with £2,000 per year (PDV just under £900,000) and was followed in 1528/9 with further papal orders dissolving another 21 small religious houses. If monasteries were not effectively administered, they were prone to become lax and corrupt. Where this occurred money was lost, standards of services dropped and monks became more self-indulgent resulting in excess eating, drinking, sport and socialising with the opposite sex. A report on a visit by the Bishop of Lincoln to Dorchester-on-Thames abbey at the periphery of his massive diocese, found that the monks spent their evenings in the common room with "women friends, best Abingdon ale and games of chess." The abbot was reported to have had up to 'five mistresses' while outside the precincts, the monks were said to enjoy hawking, hunting, frequenting taverns which sometimes involved "brawling with local youths after drink[20]."

Further evidence for this profligacy can be seen in the surviving journals[21] of William More who was prior at Worcester Cathedral between 1518-36. His income from 16 manors was equal to 25% of the priory's entire revenues which enabled him to live for the majority of the year on one of his three rural estates pursuing a life of the country gentleman which often meant entertaining members of the royal family. He also spent one month in London spending extravagantly on clothes, jewellery, embroidery, books, wine and gifts. It appears this left him little time to attend his cathedral other than at Christmas, Easter and Whitsuntide.

The trivial sounding 'Act in Restraint of Appeals 1533' has been described as the most important church statute in English constitutional history. It terminated papal jurisdiction in this country and enabled the newly created Church of England to grant Henry his wish to divorce his wife Catherine of Aragon without reference to Rome. Catherine was the daughter of the king and queen of Spain whose close alliance with the Pope made divorce impossible. In the following year, the 'Act of Supremacy 1534' anointed Henry as supreme head of the newly established Anglican Church as well as giving him one-tenth of all church income, some £30,000 a year (PDV approximately £13 million).

In the 1530's, England had about 12,000 monks, friars and nuns serving in the 563 religious houses which owned from a third to a quarter of all of the country's land. Not surprisingly this fact attracted the attention of King Henry, his money-strapped government and its chief minister Thomas Cromwell who undertook a series of investigations into their workings and wealth. Bearing in mind the desired outcome, the conclusions reached by the appointed commissioners (Messrs Layton, Leigh, Rice and Tregonwell) were not unexpected with any favourable comments being removed prior to publication. Their report, as well as highlighting financial incompetence and widespread 'superstitious practices', seemed to unduly concentrate on salacious sexual details and medical failings. For example at Carlisle, seven monks were accused of sodomy while the prior and two others were claimed to be incontinent. This paper was followed in 1535 by a survey of the incomes of all the country's religious houses, known as 'Valor Ecclesiasticus.' It found that two-thirds (66%) of them (372) had incomes of less than £200 per year (PDV £86,400),

80% less than £300 per annum (£129,600) while 16% had a yearly revenue of between £300 and £1,000 (£432,000). Only 28 or 4%, almost all of which were from the Benedictine Order, had proceeds over £1,000 with Westminster and Glastonbury Abbeys having earnings of above £3,000 (£1.3 million) - see Table 2 below. The monasteries total income was put at £163,000 a year (just over £70 million), three quarters (75%) of which came from land revenues. It was claimed less than 5% of this was spent on charity for the poor and sick with most of this going to the family and friends of the monks and support staff.

Cathedral/Abbey	Establishment	Income in 1535	Number of monks or canons
Bristol	Augustinian	£670 (£289,000)	c1340-c25; 1353-18; 1534-19
Bury St Edmunds	Benedictine	£1,656 (£715,000)	1020-20; c1260-80; 1539-43
Canterbury	Monastic cathedral	£3,233 (£1.4 million)	1080-60; 1349-80; 1537-58
Carlisle	Monastic cathedral	£577 (£249,000)	1133-26; 1379-12; 1540-23
Chester	Benedictine	£1,003 (£434,000)	1381-20; 1540-11
Chichester	Secular cathedral	£698 (£302,000)	-
Durham	Monastic cathedral	£3,138 (£1.36 million)	1251-45; 1372-56; 1539-27
Ely	Monastic cathedral	£2,134 (£922,000)	1093-72; 1349-53; 1532-37
Exeter	Secular cathedral	£1,566 (£676,000)	-
Fountains Abbey	Cistercian	£1,535 (£663,000)	1200-c50; 1380-34; 1539-32
Glastonbury Abbey	Benedictine	£3,311 (£1.43 million)	1172-72; 1377-45; 1534-52
Gloucester Abbey	Benedictine	£1,430 (£618,000)	1380-54; 1534-36
Hereford	Secular cathedral	£831 (£359,000)	-
Lichfield	Secular cathedral	£795 (£343,000)	-
Lincoln	Secular cathedral	£2,095 (£905,000)	-
Lindisfarne	Benedictine	£48	-

		(£20,700)		
Norwich	Monastic cathedral	£1,050 (£454,000)	1101-60; 1533-39	1441-56;
Osney (Oxfordshire)	Augustinian	£654 (£283,000)	1377-27; 1539-13	1445-27;
Oxford	Augustinian	£220 (£95,000)	1160-18; 1520-15	1445-18;
Peterborough Abbey	Benedictine	£1,679 (£725,000)	c1340-64; 1534-42	1350-32;
Rochester	Monastic cathedral	£444 (£192,000)	1080-22; 1534-20	1210-60;
Salisbury	Secular cathedral	£1,507 (£651,000)	-	
St Albans	Benedictine	£2,102 (£908,064)	1200-100; 1530-48	1401-54;
St Paul's	Secular cathedral	£1,119 (£483,000)	-	
Wells	Secular cathedral	£1,939 (£838,000)	-	
Westminster Abbey	Benedictine	£3,470 (£1.5 million)	c1180-80; 1534-43	1381-29;
Winchester	Monastic cathedral	£2,873 (£1.24 million)	1325-64; 1533-43	1386-46;
Worcester	Monastic cathedral	£1,106 (£478,000)	1089-50; 1534-41	1401-44;
York	Secular cathedral	£2,035 (£880,000)	-	

Table 2 shows the income of cathedrals and 11 of the important monasteries from the 1535 'Valor Ecclesiasticus' survey with present day relative values (PDV) in brackets.

These findings led in 1536 to the 'Dissolution of Monasteries Act' being passed by Parliament which resulted in all religious houses with fewer than 12 monks or nuns and receiving less than £200 per year (£86,400) being closed with their wealth and income being transferred into the King's Treasury. Cromwell's commissioners continued their work investigating the larger monasteries, ruthlessly seeking out malpractice and weaknesses. In 1538, 38 monasteries were encouraged to voluntarily surrender while a second dissolution act a year later saw the remaining ones shut down with Waltham Abbey being the final one to close in March 1540. In retrospect it was surprising how little resistance was offered. Uprisings did occur in the far north-west of England, in Lincolnshire and in the so-called unsuccessful 'Pilgrimage of Grace' in Yorkshire. The last abbot at Glastonbury, Richard Whyting and two of his monks refused to surrender their monastery and were hung, drawn and quartered for treason on nearby St Michael's Tor.

Cathedrals first felt the impact from these massive changes with a campaign to discredit their shrines. An amazing spectacle occurred in April 1538 in front of Thomas Becket's one in Canterbury Cathedral. A representative of the king ordered Becket to appear in front of the king's council in one month's time to answer a charge of treason. His subsequent non-appearance was deemed to prove the Crown's case so it was resolved that Becket should no longer be treated as a saint and his name was erased from all church service books. His remains were exhumed, burnt and his shrine was dismantled. The shrine contained an amazing 672lbs (or 305kg) of gold and silver, 1120lbs (508kgs) of silver guilt and precious stones and took a reported 16 men to remove the three-quarter ton-plus monument. Other famous shrines were treated similarly: St Swithun's silver at Winchester fetched £1,333 (£576,000); Ely's St Ethelreda's gold weighed 22lbs (10kg) and silver 318lbs (144kg) while St Hugh's shrine at Lincoln contained 164lbs (75kg) of gold, 268lbs (122kg) of silver along with countless precious pearls and stones. This started a process by which a huge amount of medieval church artwork was removed, melted down and should have produced a massive windfall for the King's Treasury. It is believed, however, that widespread corruption and pilfering from officials probably resulted in only a fifth of their value reaching its intended destination.

Other church fixtures and fittings deemed 'too-catholic' were also removed. Statues of saints were smashed, murals depicting scenes from the Bible were white-washed over whilst stained glass windows, altars and fonts were destroyed. Gold and silver crosses, candlesticks, rings, jewelled gloves, tapestries, precious metals, illuminated manuscripts and gems that encrusted library books were all displaced. Pulpitums and screens separating clergy from the congregation were taken down and Lady Chapels were demolished. In 1547, all chantry chapels were suppressed with their endowments, properties and rents going straight to the Treasury. Monastic land was sold off to the wealthy, lead was stripped from roofs, buildings were pillaged for their stone and left as empty shells to allegedly prevent them being re-occupied. Some monasteries like Bury St Edmunds were attacked and damaged by local citizens seeking revenge for years of perceived 'arrogance' and for their imposition of onerous local taxes.

As part of this process, dioceses were re-organised with cathedrals given new functions and liturgy. In May 1538, Norwich became the first monastic cathedral to be converted into a secular one or, as it is known, a cathedral of the 'New Foundation.' This was repeated at Canterbury, Carlisle, Durham, Ely, Rochester, Winchester and finally Worcester in January 1542. The reformed Canterbury was now served by a dean, 12 prebends, 12 minor canons and 6 preachers to provide for the increased importance given to providing sermons. When servants and other officers were added the new establishment totalled 134. The reconstituted cathedrals were provided with a more equitable funding arrangement whereby the wealthier ones like Canterbury, Durham and Westminster Abbey's income decreased whilst the poorer dioceses like Rochester and Carlisle were given increased allowances. The newly constituted cathedrals each pooled their revenues and paid a set salary known as a stipend to their staff – deans, canons and singers were paid £300, £40 and £6 per year (PDV £129,000, £17,200 and £2,580) respectively. The patron saints of cathedrals were also changed to exclude locally named ones and those with Catholic connections to be replaced by more generic names like Christ Church, All Saints and All Souls.

There were also proposals to create up to 18 new cathedrals with the following 28 towns being considered[22]: Colchester and Waltham (Essex); St Albans (Hertfordshire); Dunstable, Elstow and Newnham (Bedfordshire & Buckinghamshire); Osney and Thame (Oxfordshire & Berkshire); Peterborough (Northamptonshire and Huntingdonshire); Westminster (Middlesex); Leicester (Leicestershire & Rutland); Bristol and Gloucester (Gloucestershire); Fountains (Lancashire & Richmond); Bury St Edmunds (Suffolk); Chester, Shrewsbury and Wenlock (Cheshire, Shropshire & Staffordshire); Southwell, Welbeck, Worksop and Thurgarton (Nottinghamshire and Derbyshire); Launceston, Bodmin, St Germans and Plympton (Cornwell); Guisborough and Beverley (Yorkshire). The widespread disruption that this plan would have caused together with the king and his government's insatiable need for money meant only six were actually established: at the former Benedictine abbeys of Bristol, Chester, Gloucester and Peterborough whilst the cathedral status of Osney (Oxford) and Westminster Abbey lasted for a combined total of only 14 years.

The Reformation resulted in around one-third of monasteries being completely destroyed, one third survived in part mostly as ruins whilst the remainder are still used today as religious edifices. Monastic cathedrals suffered far more than secular ones although only two cathedrals, at Osney (Oxford) and Coventry (St Mary's), were completely lost. Many abbots and monks negotiated new jobs in the new regime with monks becoming canons, priors deans and abbots bishops. Nevertheless, it is believed that up to a quarter of all monks and friars lost their livelihoods with nuns effectively losing everything. Some individual monastic buildings have survived being converted for other uses but communal buildings like the cloisters, dormitory, refectory, infirmaries and kitchens generally did not.

Despite the massive fortune that taking over the monasteries land which raised about £750,000 (PDV £324 million) and the plundering of their religious artifices was expected to produce, by 1547 the king's financial situation was in a far worse state than it was before. Only a small proportion of the money raised reached the planned education and charity budgets with most going to fund wars with France and Scotland. The desperate need for ready money meant that rather than retaining land and renting it out, assets were hastily sold off on the cheap so when Henry died in January 1547, half of the monastic land had already been sold off. By 1558 only a quarter was still in Crown hands so that within a generation of the closure of the monasteries most of their former land and wealth not transferred to the newly created secular cathedrals were owned by the noblemen, gentry and merchants of the Elizabethan age.

For the 11 years following Henry VIII's death, the country and particularly the church, were in a constant state of turmoil. Henry was succeeded by his nine year old son Edward VI who was heavily reliant on his advisers, particularly the arch-Protestant churchman Archbishop Cranmer. During his six year reign the country became even more extreme and religiously intolerant which affected all aspects of church life from the liturgy, personnel, music, fixtures and fittings. The New English Bible was introduced into all churches, sermons were preached in English with Latin being outlawed and another financial crisis meant further raids on church assets. In 1550, York Minster lost all its gold and silver chalices, bread boxes, gold and silver basins, crosses with precious stones, candlesticks, goblets, ale pots and highly decorative mitres. Edward's death in July 1553 resulted in his elder half-sister Mary, daughter of Catherine of Aragon and an ardent Catholic, taking the throne. She repealed all of Edward's religious legislation, Latin services were reintroduced, Catholic clerics were released from prison to be replaced by Protestant ones including Cranmer while monastic rule was even restored to Westminster Abbey. Protestants were forced to flee to the Continent while 300 were executed becoming known as the 'Marian Martyrs.' It was difficult to find bishops who shared Mary's views, however, so when she died in November 1558, the dioceses of Carlisle, Chichester, Lincoln, Oxford, Peterborough, Salisbury and Worcester were all vacant. Her successor, the Protestant Elizabeth I, was to reverse all of Mary's changes with the mayhem caused to cathedral buildings, their personnel and possessions during this brief period (1547-58) being all too easily imagined[23].

Only superficial repairs were undertaken to rectify the extensive damage done to England's cathedrals at this time because of apathy and financial problems. Early 17th Century reports mention the poor state of repair of Gloucester, Lichfield, Norwich, Wells, Winchester and Worcester cathedrals but the two worst affected were Carlisle and Old St Paul's. And things were about to get far worse for within half a century the country was to plunge into another massive crisis.

The causes of the English Civil Wars have been much debated but it was essentially an argument over power and authority between the monarch and its parliament. In this the established church firmly supported the king as the supreme 'defender of the faith' whilst, opposing them, the parliamentarian puritans wanted to finally put an end to centuries of what they perceived to be the corrupting power and wealth of the Roman Catholic church, purging the English church of superstition and idolatry.

Contemporary accounts give a flavour of what was occurring throughout the country. Parliamentary troops on going into Canterbury Cathedral in August 1642 claimed that it was a 'stable for idols'. They destroyed the Communion table, monuments, organ, lectern, vestments, Bible and prayer books. Four months later they returned with parliamentary commissioners to smash stained glass windows, statues, the cloisters, clergy houses and the bones of saints. Oliver Cromwell, leader of the Parliamentarians, was personally responsible for defacing Peterborough Cathedral in 1643 which lost its organ, choir stalls, Katherine of Aragon's tomb, its Lady Chapel and its cloisters, which were described as being the finest in the country with its colourful medieval glass depicting all of the early kings of England.

Cathedrals that were located in cities that were not fought over tended to suffer far less than former royal strongholds. Worcester Cathedral housed 6,000 prisoners while Lichfield suffered 2,000 canon shots, was ransacked, lost its spire and lead roof leaving it in a 'ruinous state.' The utter contempt is best summed up after Old St Paul's Cathedral was taken over as a barracks. Soldiers used the communion table for eating, drinking and smoking, the ceremonial robes for play acting and even 'baptised' a horse with urine from one of their helmets.

Following the Parliamentarians victory in 1649, an Act of Parliament abolished all offices and titles relating to cathedrals resulting in up to 10,000 clergy being made unemployed and homeless. Valuable materials were removed from cathedrals and sold, their land and property was confiscated to secure loans which raised over £500,000 (PDV £93 million). This bounty was mainly used to finance Cromwell's 'New Model Army' and his navy.

Inside cathedrals, partitions were taken down as it was believed that no part of a church could be any more holy than another and to prevent clergy from 'performing their magic behind screens.' Some cathedrals were shut down during this period, others were used as preaching houses and parish churches whilst some even became stables. After Scotland joined the royalists, Carlisle suffered significant damage during the battle of Dunbar in 1650 which resulted in 3,000 Scots being held prisoners-of-war in Durham Cathedral with as many as 1,600 perishing there. The victors proposed demolishing Winchester Cathedral as it was thought irrelevant and too costly to maintain. It was only saved by a last minute local petition. Indeed a proposal in 1651 to pull down all of England's cathedrals and use the money for poor relief was debated in Parliament. Fortunately for this book, the motion was defeated!

When the so-called 'Commonwealth' era ended in 1660 with the restoration of the monarch, nowhere was this more celebrated than in the cathedrals. Its clergy were re-employed and a massive programme to restore the ruinous state of the nation's churches began. Lichfield was unusable with services having to take place in its chapter house. Its bishop gave £1,683.40 (PDV £252,000) and the canons £1,035 (£155,000) to the £9,092.08p (£1.36 million) cost of remediation.

This programme also included the building of England's first purpose-built Anglican Cathedral. The gigantic hulk which was the London cathedral of Old St Paul's had suffered a lightning strike in June 1561 losing it lofty timber spire and causing a fire which completely destroyed its timber roof. Despite temporary repairs, the cathedral fell into an abject condition. A contemporary quotation survives: to repair choir, nave, aisles, steeple, chapter house, north and south transepts would cost £31,536.29 (PDV £9.8 million) – a completely unrealistic amount of money to raise. Architect Inigo Jones undertook some short-term and controversial remedial works but its final demise came in 1666 when it was completely destroyed in the Great Fire of London. After much debate, it was decided to completely rebuild it in a classical Renaissance style which was done between 1675 and 1710 by Sir Christopher Wren at a staggering cost of £736,752 (PDV £101 million) for which he was paid £200 per year (£28,400), with most of the money raised coming from a tax on all coal imported into the capital. Its design was not without controversy and underwent several modifications during its building which considerably increased the final cost. The current nave retains its original clean, austere looks with its plain clear glass windows but the east end has been much changed by the Victorians.

The 18th Century could rightly be thought of as the nadir of English cathedral history. They were described as being small areas of "privilege and decadence, staffed by lazy, pompous clerics, drawn from genteel families who had little interest in or knowledge of ordinary people[24]." Norwich Cathedral midweek congregations were said to number only a dozen which contrasted markedly with the passion and enthusiasm of the newly formed non-Conformist sects like the Baptists, Congregationalists, Presbyterians, Quakers, Unitarians and later the Methodists. These attracted large numbers to their plain, simple churches and chapels in largely industrial, working class areas of the country. The architectural community had also fallen out of love with Gothic preferring the neo-classical Renaissance style based on ancient Rome and Greece. This indifference not only led to neglect but, even worse, produced some highly damaging cathedral restoration schemes in an attempt to tidy up the perceived disorder. Chapels, west fronts, towers, spires, fixtures and fittings as well as whole sections of cathedrals were replaced by work of dubious quality. Nowhere was this better illustrated than in the late 18th Century restoration work undertaken by James Wyatt (1747-1813), a man described by Pugin as the "pest of cathedral architecture", at Hereford, Lichfield, Salisbury and Durham. Similar controversial work was undertaken at Ely and Lincoln by James Essex although the bishops and their chapters, who commissioned these works, cannot be absolved of their share of responsibility.

Writer William Corbett described an abject service he attended at Winchester Cathedral in 1825 presided over by half a dozen men and boys in white surplices with a congregation numbering 15 women and four men. 25 years later it was reported that while weekday services at St Paul's attracted 150, Canterbury's were attended by between 25 and 53, Durham's evensong from 25 to 37 while at Peterborough just seven were present. This indifference was also reflected in the poor physical state of England's cathedrals. Winchester's roof leaked, Canterbury had broken windows and York's damp was so intrusive that services had to be suspended in the 1850's. This was partly due to two major fires in 1829 and 1840 that required £60,000 (PDV £5.4 million) to restore, funded by selling some of their London properties. St Albans abbey was in such a miserable condition that there was serious proposals to completely demolish it.

In order for a more equitable distribution of church funds and provide better facilities and services for the rapidly expanding industrial populations found mostly in the Midlands and the north of England, the Ecclesiastic Commissioners or Cathedrals Act was passed to 1840. Its purpose was to make savings of £140,000 a year (PDV £13.7 million) by reducing the number of cathedral personnel. In fact about £300,000 (£29.4 million) was saved by these measures.

In an attempt to make cathedrals more welcoming and relevant as well as to attract the working class for the first time, Sunday evening services were introduced. These were held in the heated nave, employed charismatic preachers, accompanied by choirs and music which, despite wide-scale indifference from cathedral clergy, proved very popular. Their appeal increased further with the coming of the railways attracting vast numbers of tourists in search of history, art and music. 48,000 visited St Paul's Cathedral in 1840 which increased to 71,000 five years later. This expansion in popularity enabled English cathedrals to be restored to a far higher standard and in a more sensitive style during the Victorian period.

Many English cities suffered significant air raid damage during the Second World War (1939-45). Exeter Cathedral took a direct hit, Birmingham lost its roof, Manchester a chapel whilst both London's St Paul's Cathedral and Westminster Abbey miraculously survived heavy German bombing. So important were these two buildings that Britain's war time leader Winston Churchill ordered that any incendiary bombs, which caused most of the damage, be immediately extinguished although two bombs did penetrate St Paul's roof. Only Coventry Cathedral was destroyed outright with its remains later being incorporated into its replacement church, a poignant reminder of the conflict.

9. CONCLUSIONS
Summary of answers and the English cathedral today

....

T his concluding chapter aims to summarise answers to the questions raised in the introduction and look at the English cathedral today.

Why was a cathedral built here? What was so special about this place?

History shows that once a site has been deemed sacred by one civilisation, it is likely to be similarly revered, used and developed by subsequent ones. Canterbury, London, Lincoln and York cathedral sites have all been occupied for religious purposes by the Romans, Anglo-Saxons, Normans and the English right up until the present day. Any standing churches were either adapted or, more likely, completely rebuilt on a grander scale to emphasise the new culture's superiority over its predecessor. We have seen how important it was for the early Christian missionaries to obtain and then maintain the support of regional Anglo-Saxon kings in order to spread their message. Their initial bases were established in six of the seven kingdom capitals at the time – certainly at Canterbury, London, York and Winchester; probably also at Lincoln and at Repton/Lichfield. If the king or his successor renounced their faith then Christians would be forced to leave and the region and its people would revert back to paganism. This is what happened to London in the middle of the 7th Century and is why the more stable kingdom of Kent retained the seat of the Archbishop of All England in Canterbury, a situation that remains the case to this day.

The English church has attempted throughout its history to create equal-sized, manageable and stable diocesan areas from which to administer their religion. Augustine's original vision for 16 sees, 12 in the south under London and four in the less populated north under York, was never fully materialised for political and military reasons. Major changes were undertaken by Theodore in 669 who established eight new cathedrals. Later Viking invasions, mostly affecting eastern England, meant that many were destroyed and abandoned with see headquarters being moved west to safer, isolated rural locations. This policy was later reversed following the Norman Conquest when diocesan centres were moved back to more significant urban settlements where they could be more easily defended from newly-built fortified castles.

Henry VIII created an additional six sees and cathedrals following the Reformation to address the large bishoprics of Lincoln and York whose headquarters were located on the periphery of their administration areas. The massive shifts of population following the Industrial Revolution which largely affected the Midlands and northern England, resulted in 20 new cathedrals being established between 1836 and 1927, the majority being former parish churches. The trend resumed in 2014 with the re-organisation of West Yorkshire which could ultimately effect the status of three current cathedrals.

England's break from the Church of Rome in 1533 was eventually to lead to a separate Roman Catholic diocese system which today numbers 20 cathedrals while immigration from Eastern Europe has meant the formation of 13 Orthodox cathedrals, the vast majority located in London.

Who were the patrons and organisations that commissioned their building? What were the old buildings adjoining it used for?

The patrons who commissioned the building of England's medieval cathedrals were the diocesan bishops and the monastic abbots. Like the modern day client, they were responsible for providing a suitable site, funding the project, laying down what functions the building should perform, approve its design, agree a build programme and appoint a competent designer. The patron was likely to hold forthright views on how the new cathedral should look based on others he had heard about or visited.

Bishops and abbots were rich and powerful individuals whose role in medieval society extended far beyond their ecclesiastic responsibilities. Many sat in the House of Lords and some ran large government departments because they were one of the few in medieval society who were literate and educated. Their lifestyles reflected their status. As well as living in a palace within the cathedral's grounds, they also possessed large country houses, estates and often London mansions from where they entertained extravagantly. This meant they and their church were perceived as being intrinsically part of the ruling establishment which was often to prove highly unpopular with the local populace.

The initial driving force behind the Middle Age cathedral came from monasteries, particularly those belonging to the Benedictine Order. Monasteries were isolated, self-contained communities which local people rarely attended other than on special occasions. This might include taking Holy Communion once a year or paying homage at the shrine but otherwise they were totally excluded from the cathedral's sacred east end. They took no part in the services being performed in private by the monks who were concealed behind screens, closed doors and gates.

Originally monks lived harsh, strictly controlled lives regimented around the eight canonical daily services which stretched from 2am until dusk. This changed as monasteries expanded their business and commercial interests to become wealthy, worldlier institutions. Except for the bishop, abbot or prior, all other members lived communally with cloisters linking the main monastic buildings, principally the chapter house, dormitory/lavatories and refectory/kitchen. Other ancillary buildings provided medical, working, education and hospitality facilities. With their closure in the 16th Century, many of these buildings were partially or completely demolished and adapted for other uses, the result of which can be seen today adjoining our ancient cathedrals. Many of these features were copied by secular cathedrals when they took the lead in cathedral design with the arrival of Gothic architecture from France in the 12th Century.

How much did it cost? Who paid for it to be built? Where did they get their money from?

We do know the costs of at least four English cathedrals from different eras: Salisbury Cathedral (built 1220-58) cost a total of £28,000 (PDV £23.9 million) which excluded the west end and spire; St Paul's Cathedral (1675-1710) cost £736,752 (£101 million) whilst the former parish church, which became Birmingham Cathedral (1709-25), cost £5,012 (£672,000) excluding materials and transport. Coventry Cathedral, built from 1958-62, is believed to have cost in the region of £985,000 (£24.1 million).

We saw in chapter four how bishops were entitled to one quarter of cathedral income but in reality they received a far higher percentage. This made many of them extremely rich enabling them to be the major sponsors of cathedral building in the Middle Ages. Several paid the whole cost of rebuilding their cathedrals as was the case at Exeter and Ripon whilst other bishops gave the majority of money to build extensions and alterations as happened at Ely, Winchester, Salisbury, Chichester and Durham. The rest of the money came from the cathedral's fabric fund (nominally 25% of their income), donations from clergy, monks and the wealthy, church collections and nationwide appeals.

England was an agricultural society in the Middle Ages with dioceses and monasteries owning as much as one-third of the country's land. Many possessed the entire adjoining town from which they obtained rent and taxes from property, fairs, markets and roads. Poor quality agricultural land was utilised for sheep farming with the highly prized wool being exported to Europe raising considerable wealth. Cathedrals also owned some 40% of parish tithes from which they were entitled to receive '10% of the fruits of the land' or produce in kind. Money was also received from their various religious entrepreneurial schemes – pilgrim donations to the shrines of saints, chantry chapels and the payment of indulgencies to reduce religious penalties.

Why is it shaped like it is? Why is it so big? What functions did it perform?

The phrase 'always the same yet somehow always different' could describe England's cathedrals. No two are identical: the site, date of erection, the current architectural style, the amount of available money, the patron's and designer's preferences all ensured this. Yet they all have similar characteristics: cruciform shaped for symbolic reasons usually with a central tower at the crossing, orientated east / west, clergy to the east, laity to the west, originally rigidly separated spiritually and physically by solid partitions.

Following the Norman Conquest, the modest-sized Anglo-Saxon cathedrals were ruthlessly swept away to be replaced by enormous structures comparable to anything seen in Europe which emphasised the power of the new state and its religion. Most were so large that they could accommodate the entire populace of the neighbouring town within their naves alone. These early Norman cathedrals were then constantly modified or replaced as a result of new functions, technological advances, changes to liturgy and architectural style. The shrines of saints, originally housed in crypts, were brought up into the east ends which had to be subsequently enlarged and improved. Additional chapels were needed for private worship and devotion, the most important of these were the Lady and chantry chapels in memory of the Virgin Mary and wealthy benefactors.

Who designed it? Where did the ideas come from?

The designer of the medieval cathedral was a master stonemason, invariably a laymen, highly trained and educated. He would have gained his considerable experience by travelling extensively to work on a variety of building projects and working alongside master and fellow masons. Despite claims made in the past and repeated today, it seems impossible that this specialist work could be undertaken by untrained, religious personnel.

A medieval architect would be capable of visualising the finished building at design stage before a stone has been laid and proficient at communicating this image to both patrons and builders by drawings, models and templates. He would have been familiar with the rules of proportion, geometry, contemporary design ideas and building technology. He appeared to have had no qualms about duplicating some of his fellow designers work and was likely to be influenced by his patron's competitive urge to surpass other rival cathedrals. He occasionally appeared to have stretched his ability by trying new things by trial and error because he lacked the modern-day knowledge of structural and material science. This occasionally resulted in some well-documented dramatic building failures which particularly affected foundations and central towers.

How was it erected before tower cranes etc. were invented? Who built it?

The building of a cathedral in the Middle Ages was a massive undertaking with building operatives arriving from all over England and occasionally Europe, who would probably far outnumber the local population. They all had to be housed, fed and provided with adequate working facilities. Getting sufficient materials, particularly stone and timber, was a major concern and, if not locally available, would require transporting often from as far afield as Europe at considerable cost. Other items we would currently purchase from shops and warehouses had to be manufactured, fabricated or mixed on site, for example timber lifting devices and wagons were made by the carpenter, tools by blacksmiths and mortar mixed by the mortarmen.

The medieval cathedrals were built by professional, highly trained craftsmen under the supervision of a master stonemason or occasionally a master carpenter who designed, drew and supervised its building. Often several individuals undertook this role on a project because of the lengthy build process. This conclusion is supported by hundreds of cathedral accounts from the Middle Ages showing chapters making substantial payments to lay master masons and artisans to undertake the building works.

After clearing the site, the cathedral was orientated invariably facing east determined by observing the rising sun on the cathedral's patron saint day. The foundations would be excavated and filled after the building had been set out to the agreed size. This was followed by an elaborate ceremony in which religious leaders and local dignitaries laid the first stones. Work would start at the sacred east end and progressed westwards with the nave often being completed years later once sufficient funds had been raised. A wide range of trades were needed to complete the cathedral: stone masons for the masonry, carpenters for the timberwork, plumbers for the lead roof and drainage; glaziers for the windows; tilers for the flooring; joiners for the fittings and fixtures; plasterers and decorators for the walls; sculptors for the statues and artists for the wall and ceiling paintings. The large amount of lifting and carrying required vast numbers of paid labourers.

How does it differ from European cathedrals? How has it changed since it was first built?

Tourists who have visited European cathedrals will note some fundamental differences from their English counterparts. This country's cathedrals tend to stand apart from the adjoining city in a secure, quiet oasis surrounded by ancient buildings, manicured lawns, enclosed by walls and gatehouses. The cathedral itself is generally considerably longer and not as tall, spires are rare, west fronts unelaborate and interiors more restrained.

The inside of an English cathedral we see today is a pale shadow of its former glory. Gone are the wall paintings, medieval stained glass windows, furniture, fittings, statues, books and embroidery with their rich colours, precious metals and jewellery. The stripping of their interiors was the result of a change of religion, Henry VIII's need for money to fund wars with France and Scotland, the havoc caused by his two immediate successors one an ardent Protestant the other a staunch Catholic and the 17th Century English Civil Wars. In this dispute, fought between the King and his Parliament, the established church firmly supported the monarch which meant that it suffered enormously following the subsequent Parliamentarian victory. Any cathedral with royal connections or perceived as being too catholic was sabotaged by the Protestant victors: furniture, statues, shrines, paintings, stained glass windows were smashed while chantry and Lady Chapels, cloisters and the hated division screens which separated the clergy from the laity were all largely destroyed.

The general apathy shown by most people to cathedrals and to the Gothic style in particular by the architectural profession, led to their widespread neglect in the 18th Century. Some were in such a poor state that they were seriously considered for demolition, as was the case at Winchester and St Albans with the situation being made even worse by some controversial demolitions and poor quality restoration works. This contrasted sharply with the vibrant non-Conformist religious movements that sprang up around the country at this time. What saved the English cathedrals were the introduction of more enlightened services which attracted for the first time congregations from a wider section of society and, with the coming of the railways, more tourists interested in visiting the county's historic buildings. This was eventually to lead to all of this country's medieval cathedrals being restored to a high quality during the Victorian era.

Is it still used today?

Cathedrals are still central to the three main sects of the Christian faith in England, being the headquarters and the most important church in their respective dioceses. Today most Anglican cathedrals will hold at least two daily services, double this number on a Sunday and even more at Easter and Christmas with their music and choirs being renowned throughout the world. Cathedrals also provide a venue for celebration and mourning on a local, regional and national basis as well as hosting numerous arts, literary and musical events. Each Anglican cathedral is run independently by a chapter of clergy and lay persons under the direction of a dean. They are tasked with raising the considerable finances required to administer and maintain their cathedral with the money coming from donations from the congregation, visitors, legacies, trading, investments, appeals, government and national lottery grants.

In 1872 the Church of England was by far the country's largest landowner owning some 2.2 million acres most of which was rented to farmers and has subsequently been sold off. As recently as 2012 their total assets were put at around £5.5 billion which annually raised £146 million. Half the assets are held in stocks and shares, over £400 million in worldwide real estate and over £320 million in commercial property. The church still owns over 105,000 acres of agricultural land in this country and some 1,800 residential properties in central London.

The arrival of immigrants from outside Europe particularly since the 1960's with their different faiths and the rise of secularism has changed the religious composition of the country. The 2011 Census found that, while 59.4% of the population stated that they are Christian, 24.7% said that they had no religion, 5% were Muslim, 1.5% Hindu, 2.2% other religions while 7.2% were unknown.

Today England's cathedrals have never been more popular attracting record numbers of native and overseas visitors. This has led to them having to house all the trappings of the modern day tourist industry: souvenir shops, restaurants, toilets, coach parks and signage. Financing their high maintenance and running costs has led to some controversial decisions like charging for admission.

A social survey undertaken at the turn of the Second Millennium found that over 25% of the population had visited a cathedral during the previous twelve months, far higher than those attending a football match. Our enduring passion for, and continuing sense of wonder at, the medieval cathedral means that its patron, the designer, its builders, the state and its religion would all consider that their church had accomplished precisely what they had all set out to achieve.

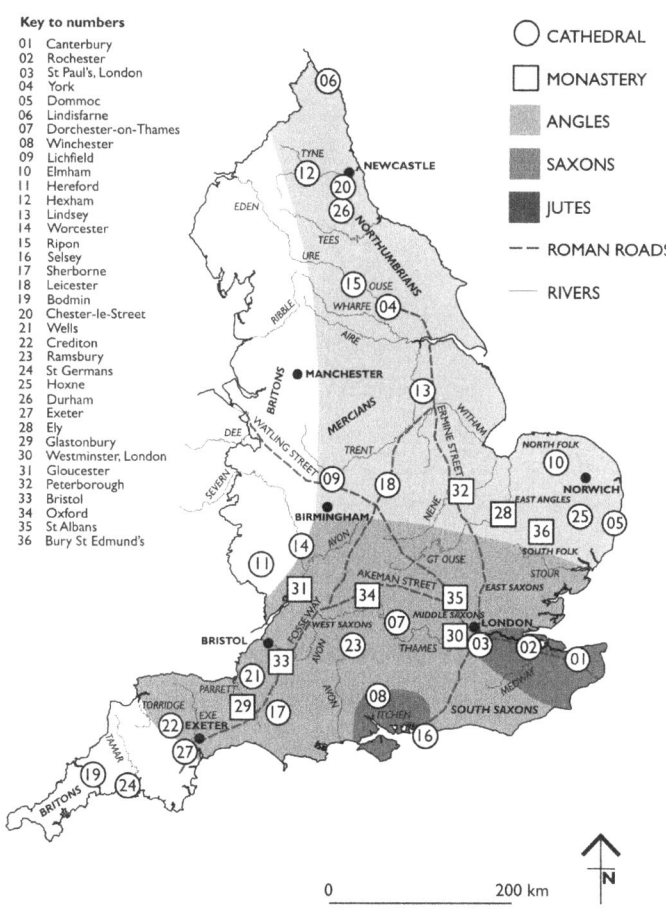

Key to numbers

01 Canterbury
02 Rochester
03 St Paul's, London
04 York
05 Dommoc
06 Lindisfarne
07 Dorchester-on-Thames
08 Winchester
09 Lichfield
10 Elmham
11 Hereford
12 Hexham
13 Lindsey
14 Worcester
15 Ripon
16 Selsey
17 Sherborne
18 Leicester
19 Bodmin
20 Chester-le-Street
21 Wells
22 Crediton
23 Ramsbury
24 St Germans
25 Hoxne
26 Durham
27 Exeter
28 Ely
29 Glastonbury
30 Westminster, London
31 Gloucester
32 Peterborough
33 Bristol
34 Oxford
35 St Albans
36 Bury St Edmund's

○ CATHEDRAL
□ MONASTERY
ANGLES
SAXONS
JUTES
– – ROMAN ROADS
— RIVERS

0   200 km   N

Figure 1 – LOCATION: A map of England before the 1066 Norman Conquest showing medieval cathedrals and significant monasteries along with Anglo-Saxon kingdoms, their people, major rivers and the main Roman roads. These factors affected the siting of this country's ancient cathedrals.

Figure 2 – LOCATION: Choosing an imposing site for your church. Nowhere is this better illustrated by the one selected at Durham by the displaced monks from Lindisfarne in 995AD for their new monastery as viewed from the air and the river Wear.

Figure 3 – LOCATION: The massive structures of both Canterbury (top) and Lincoln (bottom) cathedrals demonstrate how even today they dominate their respective cities. Imagine how much more this would have been the case when they were first built on this scale at the end of the 11th Century.

Figure 4 – DESIGN: Cathedrals built on flat terrain could enhance their presence by adding towers and spires. Most of the latter have long disappeared but the ones at Salisbury (top) and Lichfield (bottom) cathedrals are notable exceptions.

Figure 5 – DESIGN: Photographs showing the differences between Romanesque architecture in Ely Cathedral nave (top) built from c1090-1197 and the later Decorated Gothic style at Exeter Cathedral (bottom) from 1308-82.

Figure 6 – LOCATION: Two surviving former Anglo-Saxon temporary cathedrals. St Martin's Church, Canterbury (left) is believed to have been used by Augustine as his cathedral from c597 until around 602 when a more suitable replacement was completed nearby while (right) St Peter-on-the Wall chapel, Bradwell-on-Sea, Essex was the home of the Bishop of London from around 654 until 675.

Figure 7 – DESIGN: St Albans Cathedral (left) showing an older Romanesque bay to the right alongside a later Gothic one. York has some of the county's finest surviving stained glass. Three of the 117 panels (centre) from the minster's massive 23.3 metre tall by 9.5 metre wide Perpendicular style east window erected 1405-8 by Coventry glazier John Thornton and (right) the east window dating from c1330 in a Decorative style by master mason Ivo de Raghton with the glazing probably by Robert Kettlebarn.

Figure 8 – DESIGN: The west front is the public façade of a cathedral being its main entrance with Peterborough's (top), built c1193-1230, being unusually grand for a former abbey. The cathedral also has a fully developed fan-vaulted ceiling (above left) dating from around 1496 to 1508 probably by John Wastell, who worked on Kings' College chapel in Cambridge. Peterborough also possesses the only surviving timber painted ceiling (above centre and right) dating from 1230-50 including a depiction of geometry, one of the liberal arts.

Figure 9 – DESIGN: Wells Cathedral west front (c1230-60) by Thomas Norreys which house the 350 or so life-sized or larger statues that were originally highly gilded and decorated. Most of the screen consists of kings, biblical and religious figures (top left) but inside the cathedral there are some wonderful secular caricatures' such as the the owner punishing the thief which forms part of the Grape Stealers series (bottom left) and the man with a toothache (bottom right), both of which can be found in the south transept.

Figure 10 – DESIGN: Exeter Cathedral has some of the best preserved fixtures and fittings including the oldest bishop's throne (centre above). It has the most extensive surviving misericords dating from the 13th Century which includes (top left) a purported portrayal of King Herod sitting in a bucket of water to relieve the symptoms of his haemorrhoids.

Figure 11 – DESIGN: Some designers often made sculptures of themselves and built them into their edifices as Thomas Witney did at Exeter Cathedral (left). The Great Model of St Paul's Cathedral (right) shows Christopher Wren's third of his five design proposals and would have been used to demonstrate his proposals to the layperson.

Figure 12 – DESIGN: Liverpool's religious divide inspired the building of two imposing cathedrals with differing architectural styles both of which took over a century to complete from their inception. The traditional Anglican cathedral completed only in 1978 was by architect G.G. Scott and is currently the seventh largest church in the World with the image on the right showing it being built in 1937.

Figure 13 – DESIGN: Liverpool's Roman Catholic Metropolitan Cathedral (left) built to an innovative circular design is by Frederick Gibberd. An even more ambitious scheme by Sir Edwin Lutyens, which would have created the second largest church in the World, the model of which is shown right. Spiralling costs meant that only the crypt was completed and sits below the current cathedral.

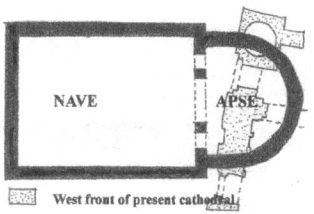
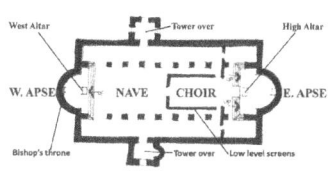

Figure 14 – PURPOSE: (left) a plan of the 7th Century Anglo-Saxon cathedral at Rochester Cathedral showing its relationship to the Norman west front and (right) Canterbury Cathedral probably from the 10th Century. Note how in the later both east and west ends were used by the clergy in contrast to later Norman churches where the liturgical focus was exclusively on the eastern arm.

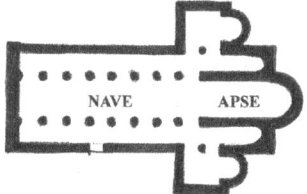
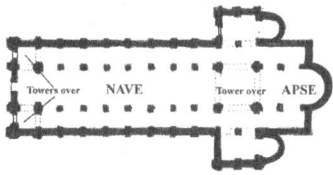

Figure 15 – PURPOSE: Two typical examples of cathedral plans from the early Norman period. Old Sarum, Salisbury (left) built 1075-92 whose outline still survives on the ground with Canterbury built 1071-77 (right).

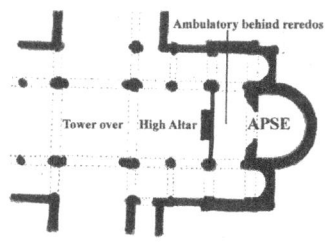
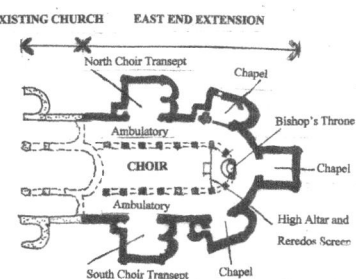

Figure 16 – PURPOSE: Two ways of improving access and circulation to early Norman cathedral east end shrines and apses. At Hereford (left) a simple solution was obtained by moving the High Altar one bay west whilst at Canterbury (right) it was achieved by building a large extension for the ambulatory.

Key to Numbers, Letters and Shading

1	Galilee porch
2	Aisle
3	Nave
4	Rood screen
5	Pulpitum
6	Choir
7	High Altar
8	Shrine
9	Chapel
10	Lady Chapel
11	North Transept
12	South Transept
13	Ambulatory
14	Slype passageway
15	Chapter House
16	Cloister Garth
17	Dorter/Reredorter over Crypt
18	Kitchen
19	Frater over Cellars
20	Priory
T	Tower over

Figure 17 – PURPOSE: A typical plan of a late Middle Age monastic cathedral with adjoining Benedictine monastery buildings showing how the church was configured before the Reformation. Read in conjunction with the glossary found in Appendix A.

Figure 18 – PURPOSE: Lady Chapels were largely destroyed by the Puritans following their victory over the Royalists in the English Civil Wars. The one at Ely Cathedral is a fine, rare survivor.

Figure 19 – PURPOSE: Hereford Cathedral's unique 'chained' library (left). A reconstruction of a medieval shrine (right) for St. Alban, England's first Christian martyr, in the cathedral and city that still bears his name.

Figure 20 – PURPOSE: Central to monastic life were the cloisters with the distinctive one at Gloucester Cathedral (left) built c1370-1412 being one of England's finest. Vicars' Close at Wells Cathedral (right) dates from the 14th Century and is therefore one of Europe's oldest residential roads.

Figure 21 – PURPOSE: Two views of settlements damaged and abandoned following the 'Dissolution of the Monasteries' in the 16th Century. Glastonbury Abbey (left) was a cathedral from 1195-1218 and when closed was the second wealthiest monastery in the country. Fountains Abbey in North Yorkshire was considered for cathedral status by Henry VIII which has extensive remains of its cellar (right) which originally had the monks' dormitory above.

Figure 22 – BUILDING: A drawing depicting a medieval cathedral building site. Note the Gothic style of architecture, the temporary shuttering supporting the recently completed arches, the semi-complete flying buttresses, closed timber roof, scaffolding and in the distance a windlass lifting machine.

Figure 23 – BUILDING: Two drawings probably by St Albans monk and chronicler Matthew Paris (c1200-59) showing the king instructing the master mason, who is shown holding his square and compass. The illustrations give a good idea of some contemporary building equipment.

Figure 24 – BUILDING: Two images showing building operations in the 15th Century. (Left) shows a masons' workshop, walls under construction and labourers transporting materials with barrows and stretchers while (right) illustrates masons working and laying stones assisted by a mortarman and labourers.

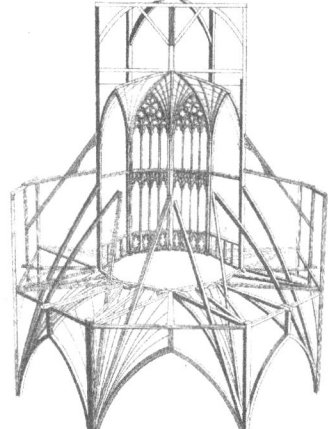

Figure 25 – BUILDING: Details of the amazing central crossing octagon tower at Ely Cathedral built 1322-46 by master carpenter William Hurley as illustrated in C.A. Hewett's book 'English Cathedral Carpentry' (left) and as viewed from below (right) showing later Victorian decorations.

Figure 26 – BUILDING: The principal lifting device used in Middle Age building operations was the windlass. The one (left) is in the base of Salisbury Cathedral spire dating from when the cathedral was built but was reassembled in 1762. A view from inside Salisbury Cathedral spire (right) said to weigh over 6,000 tons showing the permanent scaffolding used during its erection.

Figure 27 – POST-COMPLETION: The iconic Second World War image (left) of St Paul's Cathedral under attack on 29th December 1940 during the London Blitz and miraculously surviving while (right) Coventry Cathedral was not so lucky. The ruins are a poignant reminder of the conflict here photographed next to the replacement cathedral built 1956-62.

Figure 28 – POST-COMPLETION: The Roman Catholic church has 20 cathedrals in England with its headquarters being Westminster Cathedral (left) built in a striking Byzantine style by architect J.F. Bentley to contrast with the nearby Westminster Abbey. England is the home of 13 Eastern Orthodox cathedrals with St. Sophia (right) in west London being the mother house of the Greek Orthodox church for the whole of western Europe.

Figure 29 – POST COMPLETION: Westminster Abbey, London (top) showing its close proximity to the seat of government signified by 'Big Ben' and the Houses of Parliament with the Anglican parish church St Margaret sandwiched between. The Millennium Bridge spanning the river Thames and opened in June 2000 gives another dramatic view of St Paul's Cathedral (bottom).

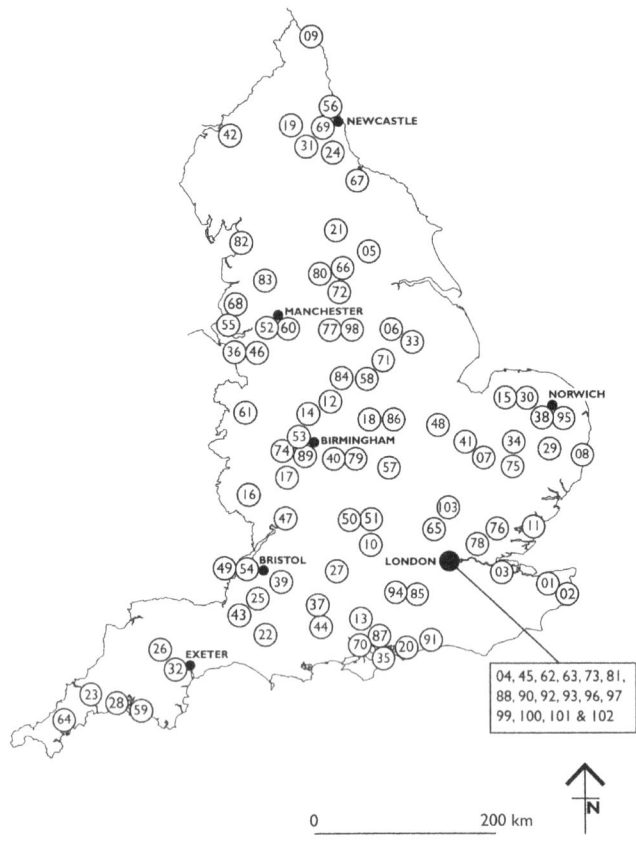

Figure 30 – LOCATION: A map of England showing its 103 current and former cathedrals as listed in Appendix B. The numbers refer to when the cathedral was first founded, 01 being the oldest, 103 the most recent.

...………………………...…………………………………………

Appendix A – A Glossary of Terms Used in this Book

Read in conjunction with the cathedral plan shown on *figure 17*. Good surviving examples are listed in the relevant sections.

Abbey A monastery church whose head is an abbot (in a male establishment) or an abbess (in a female one). Where a bishop resides, the monastery and its monks are led by a prior.

Aisle A side passage for access and processions running alongside the nave, transepts and presbytery separated by arcades of columns and arches. Usually aisles are shorter in height than the main body of a church to allow for a high-level gallery (triforium) and windows (clerestory) which admit daylight into the centre of a cathedral.

Ambulatory A walkway for processions around the presbytery at the east end of a cathedral.

Anglican A denomination of Christian Protestantism which dates from the 16th Century teachings of the German monk Martin Luther (1483-1546) and is particularly popular in the world's English speaking countries. The Anglican Church of England was founded in 1534 following its split from Roman Catholicism a year earlier when a dispute arose between the Pope of Rome and King Henry VIII over his desire to divorce his first wife, Catherine of Aragon, daughter of the influential king and queen of Spain.

Apse The termination of the east end of a cathedral which is either semi-circular or semi-octagonal in shape, a feature first used in Roman basilicas.

Archbishop The head of a group of dioceses. The Church of England has two archbishops based in Canterbury and York.

Ashlar Rectangular blocks of stone, usually with one smooth dressed face.

Augustinian A monastic order introduced into England at the end of the 11th Century based on the teachings of St Augustine (354-430AD), a north African bishop. Six English cathedrals (Bristol, Carlisle, Osney, Oxford, Portsmouth and Southwark) were originally monasteries served by canons from this order. It should not be confused with Augustine and his followers who arrived in 597 to attempt to reorganise England under Church of Rome control.

Basilica   Originally a Roman court building later used as a model for early Roman churches. Today it is used to describe a large church of significant importance, e.g. St Peter's Basilica in Rome.

Bay   A repeating unit of building usually separated by vertical columns. Above the arches separating the nave and the aisle in a cathedral, is the triforium gallery and clerestory windows *(see figure 7)*.

Bede Venerable Bede (c673-735), an English monk from Monkwearmouth (Sunderland) monastery who wrote the 'Ecclesiastical History of the English People' in around 731 and on which much of our knowledge of the early church in this country is based.

Benedictine The original and most influential western monastic order based on the teachings of St Benedict of Nursia (c480-543) which arrived in England in the first half of the 7th Century. Monks were isolated from the outside world, required to pray at least eight times a day and gave vows of celibacy and poverty. The Normans reinforced and expanded the Benedictine rule in England which reached its zenith in around 1200.

Buttress   The thickening of a masonry wall designed to resist lateral forces from arches, roofs and ceiling vaults. A flying buttress is free-standing except where it connects to the wall at the thrust points and became a significant feature of Gothic architecture.

Campanile A free standing bell tower, a fine surviving example can be seen at Chichester Cathedral.

Canon (secular) A priest who served in a secular cathedral, not taking monastic vows and who usually possessed at least one prebend which financially supported him.

Canon Regular   A priest who lived and served in a monastery, for example in the Augustinian order.

Cathedral The church where the bishop has his 'cathedra' or seat. The oldest surviving example of a bishop's throne is the one in Exeter Cathedral which dates from 1312.

Chancel   The complete end of a church east of the main crossing or specifically the area around the High Altar.

Chantry chapel   A sponsored chapel where regular services were held to pray for the souls of the chantry's patron and his family. Despite being closed during the Reformation, 42 chantry chapels survive in English cathedrals, nine at

Winchester and four each at Exeter and Lincoln. Fine examples can be seen at St Albans where Abbot Ramryge chapel dates from 1521 and Henry VII's in Westminster Abbey.

Chapter House   The meeting room for the chapter, the group responsible for running the cathedral or monastery. Originally the place where a chapter of St Benedict rules were read to the assembled monks. Good surviving examples can be found at Lichfield, Lincoln, Salisbury, Wells, York and Worcester, the oldest.

Choir   Strictly speaking the area from where services are sung and not the whole of the eastern arm previously referred to as the 'quire' (see chancel, presbytery or sanctuary). The choir is frequently located under or west of the central crossing hence increasing the area of the presbytery.

Christianity   The world's largest religion based on the life and teachings of Jesus Christ, a Jewish prophet who lived in modern Palestine/Israel from around 7BC to 33AD, as depicted in the 'New Testament' of their sacred book, the Holy Bible. The Bible also includes the earlier 'Old Testament' which is a collection of old Hebrew writings predicting the arrival of a Messiah. Christianity has split into the main denominations of Roman Catholicism, Eastern Orthodoxy and Protestantism. The Eastern Orthodox church is the most conservative which means some of their churches still retain several features removed from English cathedrals following the Reformation: wall paintings, colourful images, the use of candles and incense, the altar concealed from congregation by a screen through which only the clergy can enter. Some have no pews, with the congregation standing except for the infirm.

Church of England   The official established religion of England and headquarters of the worldwide Christian Anglican community.

Cistercians Founded in 1098 in Citreaux in Burgundy (France), the so-called 'white monks' (after their clothing) arrived in England in the 12ᵗʰ Century to reinforce the original rules of St Benedict. Known for their austere and simplistic lifestyle, they occupied barren, rural locations developing sheep farming which provided their main source of income. Their isolation away from centres of population prevented any of their abbeys becoming cathedrals and led to the widespread destruction of their monasteries.

City In the past it was always assumed that a town had to have an Anglican cathedral before it could be described as a city. Since governments have taken over the role of awarding city status this is no longer the case. Today England has 42 Anglican cathedrals but 51 cities - Blackburn, Bury St Edmunds,

Guildford, Rochester and Southwell all have cathedrals but are not cities; meanwhile Bath, Brighton, Cambridge, Kingston-Upon-Hull, Lancaster, Leeds, Nottingham, Plymouth, Preston, Salford, Southampton, Stoke-on-Trent, Sunderland and Wolverhampton are cities but do not have an Anglican cathedral.

Clerestory High level windows above the nave, transepts and presbytery which admit daylight into the centre of a cathedral.

Cloisters A covered passageway originally glazed around an open quadrangle or garth usually on the warmer south side of the nave used for study and to link the monastery's main communal buildings. Good examples can be seen at Norwich, Worcester and particularly the fan-vaulted one at Gloucester *(see figure 20)*.

Close The precinct containing the bishop's palace, deanery and other residences found in a secular cathedral. Fine examples can be viewed at Salisbury Cathedral and the Vicars Close at Wells Cathedral *(see figure 20)*.

Collegiate A church served by a college of priests who live more independently and flexibly than monks in a traditional monastery. The cathedrals at Ripon and Southwell were served in this way.

Crossing Where the north/south and east/west arms of a cruciform shaped church cross, most frequently occupied by a central tower. Of England's ancient cathedrals, only Exeter does not have this feature.

Cruciform Cross shaped (see Latin cross).

Crypt A subterranean or partly underground area usually below the church's east end which in the past was used for burials. Fine examples of Anglo-Saxon crypts survive at Ripon and Hexham, Norman ones can be found at Canterbury, Gloucester, Rochester, Winchester and Worcester. The Renaissance cathedral at St Paul's in London has a crypt that has roughly the same footprint as the cathedral above.

Diocese The ecclesiastical area under the jurisdiction of a bishop (the terms see or bishopric can also be used).

Dorter A monastery's dormitory or sleeping hall.

East end The entire arm of a church east of the central crossing which contains the most sacred elements including the High Altar.

Effigy A horizontal stone statue on the tomb of the interned.

Eucharist   The ceremony known as Holy Communion by which Christians share bread and wine symbolising the body and blood of Jesus Christ.

Feretory   Refers to the place where the churches main shrine is housed, usually behind the High Altar. In the past it referred to a container where the relics of saints were kept.

Font   A basin used in the baptism ceremony.

Frater   A monastery's dining hall or refectory.

Galilee   A chapel or vestibule enclosing the porch at the main entrance of a cathedral, usually at the west end.

Gothic   The architectural style originating and fully developed in France characterised by pointed arches, ribbed vaults and flying buttresses enabling taller, more slender walls with larger windows to be built. Dating from approximately 1189 until c1558, the Gothic period is divided in England into the following styles: Early English 1189-1307 (typified by grouped, tall elongated lancet windows separated by slender masonry); Decorated 1307-77 (flamboyant, geometric window tracery), Perpendicular 1377-1485 (large windows sub-divided vertically and horizontally by straight tracery and glazing bars) and Tudor 1485-1558 with Renaissance details inserted into otherwise Perpendicular Gothic structures.

Typical Gothic windows: Early English (left); Decorated (centre) and Perpendicular (right).

Good surviving examples of Early English: Salisbury (finest complete example of the style); Durham (eastern transept, the so-called 'Chapel of the Nine Altars); Hereford (Lady Chapel); Lichfield (nave, transepts, chapter house and west front); Lincoln (main transepts, nave, central tower, Galilee porch, chapter house and retro-choir); Peterborough (western façade); Ripon (western façade); Wells (nave, double transepts, western bays of the choir and west front); Westminster Abbey (east arm, transepts and five bays of the nave, chapter house); Winchester (retro-choir); Worcester (choir); York (transepts and windows).

Decorated: Exeter (finest complete example of the style); Bristol (choir); Carlisle (east end); Ely (central octagon tower); Lincoln (central tower); Westminster Abbey (cloisters); Worcester (nave, cloisters and central tower); York (stained glass).

Perpendicular: Bath Abbey (complete example of late Perpendicular); Canterbury (nave and central tower); Gloucester (largest windows of the period, central tower with flying buttresses and Lady Chapel); Peterborough (retro-choir with fan vaulted ceiling); Westminster Abbey (western part of nave in mixed styles and chapel of Henry VII); Winchester (Perpendicular veneer on Romanesque nave and choir).

Guild   An association of merchants or artisans undertaking the same trade.

High Altar The main focus of Christian worship, originally a table on which sacrifices were made, today used to celebrate the Eucharist or Holy Communion.

Holy Communion   See Eucharist

Iconoclasm The act of breaking religious images.

Lady Chapel   A chapel built to honour the Virgin Mary, Jesus Christ's mother. She is an important figure in the Roman Catholic faith, less so for Anglicans which is why many were demolished during the Reformation. Fine surviving examples can be seen at Ely *(see figure 18)* and Lichfield cathedrals.

Latin cross The most common shape for an English cathedral. Symbolic as Christians believe that Jesus Christ was crucified on a similar shaped cross.

Magna Carta   A charter written in 1215 which defines the authority and relationship between the monarch (King John), his barons and the Church which was later incorporated into English law. Two of the four surviving documents are housed in Lincoln and Salisbury cathedrals.

Medieval   In this book, I have used the term 'Medieval' to cover the whole period from the Roman era in 43AD to the middle of the 16th Century. Westminster Abbey is arguably the single most impressive medieval building in England.

Middle Ages   I have used the term 'Middle Ages' specifically for the years from the Norman Conquest in 1066 to around 1550 with the beginning of the Renaissance period.

Minster   An imprecise term dating from Anglo-Saxon times for an important, large church. Its name survives in a number of northern churches, for example at Beverley and York.

Misericord A highly decorated, hinged tip-up seat in the choir with a ledge underneath which, when the seat is raised, helps support the user during long periods of standing. The oldest complete set are the 48 which survive at Exeter and date from 1230-60 *(see figure 10)*.

Mitred Abbeys   A monastery where its abbot was entitled to sit alongside the 17 bishops in the House of Lords, the upper chamber of the governing Houses of Parliament. In the Middle Ages there were 27 so-called mitred abbeys of which only four (Gloucester, Peterborough, St Albans and Westminster Abbey) survived as cathedrals. Seven remain partially or completely in use: Crowland, Malmesbury, Selby, Shrewsbury, Tewkesbury, Thorney and Waltham. The rest at Abingdon, Bardney, Battle, Bury St Edmunds, Canterbury St Augustine's, Cirencester, Colchester, Evesham, Holme St Benet's, Glastonbury, Ramsey, Reading, Tavistock, Winchcombe, Winchester Hyde Abbey and York St Mary's have completely or largely been destroyed.

Modern   The architectural style in England from 1914 to the present day.

Nave The main body of a church, most frequently the western arm used to accommodate the congregation or laity.

Niche   A recess in a wall, often used to house statues etc.

Normanesque   See Romanesque.

Parish   A sub-division of a diocese.

Pound   The pound sterling (£) is the British unit of currency which comprises of 100 pence (p). All monies quoted in this book have been converted to this currency.

Prebend   A property or income source which financially supports a canon in a secular cathedral. A prebendary is therefore a canon holding a prebend.

Prelate   A high ranking ecclesiastic official.

Presbytery The eastern arm of a church, including the choir, reserved for the clergy or, more particularly, the area between the choir and the High Altar. In Roman Catholicism, a presbytery is a priest's (presbyter) residence.

Present day value (PDV)   To enable monetary comparisons to be made over the years covered in this book, I have attempted to provide a present day value (PDV) for previous commodity, wage and project costs based on the purchasing power of £1 in 2013 which in 1270 was =£855; 1470=£675; 1670=£145; 1870=£85. Wages and project costs would have been considerably higher, as much as x35 times, for 'economic status' and 'prestige value' reasons. For example, it is probable that St Paul's Cathedral built at the turn of the 18th Century for a staggering three-quarters of a million pounds would today have cost far closer to the £800 million it cost to build the new national football stadium at Wembley rather than the £101 million using the above factors. See measuringworth.com website for a full discussion on the subject.

Priory   A monastic house whose head is a prior (male) or prioress (female) as opposed to an abbot or abbess.

Pro-cathedral   A provisional or temporary cathedral.

Pulpit   An elevated dais built of stone or timber dating from the late Middle Ages when preaching sermons became increasingly popular in English churches.

Pulpitum   A stone screen containing a central doorway which separates the choir from the nave used in both monastic and secular cathedrals. The gallery above was eventually used for preaching, hence the term pulpit and occasionally also supports the church organ.

Puritans   A 16th Century term used for Protestant reformers who wanted to 'purify' the Church of England from the perceived failings of Roman Catholicism. They later split and formed several non-Conformist religious sects.

Reformation   The term used for the 16th Century split when the newly formed Church of England left the Roman Catholic Communion with the king of England becoming its supreme head. As part of this process all of the country's monasteries were shut down with their lands, buildings and assets being sold off with the proceeds going to the Royal Treasury. This Act was known as the 'Dissolution of the Monasteries.' Good examples of a monastic ruin can be found at Fountains and Rievaulx in North Yorkshire, Glastonbury, Bury St Edmunds or one of the other partly destroyed mitred abbeys.

Renaissance   The term used to describe the reintroduction of Classic Greek and Roman architecture that started in Italy and spread throughout Europe, arriving in England during the 16th Century. The period is divided in this country into Elizabethan (1558-1603), Jacobean (1603-25), Stuart (1625-1702) and Georgian (1702-1830). The finest example of the style is St Paul's Cathedral in London with the nave retaining its original characteristics.

Reredorter The monastic communal lavatories usually located next to the dormitory.

Reredos   A painted or sculptured screen placed behind or above the High Altar frequently separating it from the main shrine. Good examples survive at St Albans, Southwark and Winchester.

Retro-choir A square ambulatory in a cathedral located behind the High Altar.

Roman Catholic   The largest denomination of the Christian faith whose head is the Pope with its headquarters in the Vatican City, Rome, Italy.

Romanesque

The architectural style of the Norman period in England (hence Normanesque or Anglo-Norman) dating from around 1050 to c1189, characterised by thick masonry walls derived from Roman architecture with semi-circular window and door heads consisting of rows of sculptured, ornate chevrons as illustrated. Includes the Transitional period (c1154-89) where Gothic style pointed arches were introduced into essentially Romanesque structures. (Left) a Romanesque door at Lincoln Cathedral.

Good surviving examples of Romanesque include: Durham (finest complete cathedral of the style particularly choir, transepts and western towers); Bristol (the rectangular chapter house); Canterbury (crypt); Chester St Johns Baptist Church (despite being a much altered former cathedral, it gives a rare insight into what a modest-sized Norman cathedral would have looked like); Chichester (the nave); Ely (nave and transepts); Norwich (nave, transepts, choir and apsidal chapels); Peterborough (fine interior including the only surviving original painted timber ceiling); Rochester (crypt, nave and western door); St Albans (transepts, choir and the only standing central tower); Southwell (nave, transepts and towers); Winchester (transepts, tower, choir and nave); Worcester (crypt, transepts and circular chapter house).

For the Transitional era: Chichester (retro-choir).

Rood   A cross or crucifix hanging above the entrance to the presbytery. Up until the Reformation, a rood screen carried the rood in monastic abbeys and cathedrals, separating the laity in the nave from the clergy in the presbytery (see also pulpitum). This division was extremely unpopular with 17th Century Puritans which resulted in their widespread removal. The only cathedral rood screen to survive this purge is the stone one found in St Albans Cathedral.

Sacristy   A room where sacramental vessels are stored.

Sanctuary   The area around the main altar in the eastern arm of the church.

Slype   A passageway leading out of the cloisters usually between the chapter house and the south transept.

Spire   A conical or octagonal shaped timber or stone feature built on top of a tower. The tower and spire are collectively known as a steeple. Few survive with Lichfield's three, Norwich and the tallest at Salisbury being the exceptions *(see figure 4)*.

Stalls   Choir seats frequently canopied used by the clergy or monks. Good examples can be viewed at Carlisle, Chester, Ely and Gloucester.

Stucco   A lime plaster covering a wall, often painted. If decorated when the plaster is still wet, it is known as a fresco.

Tracery   Ornamental masonry used to sub-divide a window. Horizontal members are known as transoms, vertical ones mullions.

Transept   The cross arms of a cruciform shaped church usually orientated north/south to provide additional space for worshippers and for east facing chapels.

Triforium   A high-level window-less gallery running around the nave, transepts and presbytery usually adjacent to the roof of the aisle.

Vaulting   A ceiling formed of stone arches, most simply a tunnel or barrel vault with a fan-vault being its most sophisticated, built independently below the main roof structure. Fine examples of fan vaulting can be seen in Gloucester's cloisters and Peterborough's retro-choir *(see figure 8)*.

Vicars   Today a Church of England parish priest. The name derives from 'vicarious', a deputy or substitute for a superior, as vicars originally stood in for cathedral canons to carry out their church service obligations.

Victorian/Edwardian   The architectural style in England from 1830 until the outbreak of World War I roughly equating to the reigns of Queen Victoria (1837-1901) and Edward VII (1901-10). The period included both Renaissance and Gothic Revival styles, of which Truro Cathedral is an example of the latter.

Appendix B – England's 103 Current and Former Cathedrals

This section contains a brief history of the city, the diocese, any former cathedrals, along with a description of the current cathedral including main build dates (c=circa or about), style, architect/designer (if known) and notable features. The numbers refers to when the cathedral was first founded, 01 being the oldest, 103 the most recent.

England's 42 Anglican Cathedrals

74. Birmingham Cathedral (Cathedral status 1905-present, built 1709-25, extended 1883/4). Birmingham, England's second largest city, grew rapidly during the Industrial Revolution in the 18th and 19th centuries mainly due to engineering. To reflect this increased importance, the former Georgian parish church of St Philip became a cathedral in 1905. It was built 1709-25 as a preaching house in a Baroque style to a design by Thomas Archer and cost £5,012 (PDV £672,000) with benefactors donating the materials and paying the transport costs. It was extended eastwards by J.A. Chatwin in 1883/4 to provide more space in the chancel. The cathedral lost its main roof during the Second World War.

83. Blackburn Cathedral (Cathedral status 1926-present, built 1820-6, rebuilt and extended 1831-1995). Blackburn's population grew rapidly during the Industrial Revolution due largely to textile manufacturing. The current site has been used for religious worship since before the Norman Conquest with the present cathedral being the former parish church of St Mary the Virgin. Built 1820-6 by John Palmer, its nave of five bays, north and south aisles and western tower have been incorporated into the current church. A fire in 1831 resulted in a partial rebuilding before it became a cathedral in 1926. An eastward extension designed by W.A. Forsythe was commenced in 1933 involving an aisled choir terminating in an apse, which subsequently become Jesus chapel, with large north and south aisled transepts. A great lantern tower at the crossing was never fully implemented, being completed in a more modest style by Laurence King in the early 1980's. Structural problems meant parts had to be rebuilt in the following decade.

80. Bradford Cathedral (Cathedral status 1919-present, built 1360-1508, rebuilt and extended 1615-1965). Bradford population increased rapidly in the 18th and 19th centuries because of its textile manufacturing. The cathedral's site has been used for religious purposes since Anglo-Saxon times with the oldest parts of the current church, the southern arcade, dating from the early 13th Century. A fire destroyed the church in 1327 and it was rebuilt in stages from

1360 with the nave and aisles finished in 1411 and the west tower between 1493 and 1508. Remarkably the roof was thatched until 1724. The south or Bolling chapel was replaced following a 1615 collapse and the south porch was added in 1833. Extensive restoration works were undertaken in 1860 and 1896-9, the later by TH & F Healey. Following the former parish church's raise in status to a cathedral in 1919, Sir Edward Maufe undertook a series of works between 1951 and 1965 involving new rooms to the north and south of the west tower and extending the east end by three bays. In 2014, Bradford became a sub-division within the newly created diocese of West Yorkshire and the Dales although it retains for the time being its cathedral status.

49. Bristol Cathedral (Cathedral status 1542-1836 and 1897-present; built 1220-1515 and 1868-88). Bristol was one of the four wealthiest cities in England from the 13th Century until the Industrial Revolution 500 years later, developing around its port. Only the chapter house and abbey gatehouse remains from the period following its foundation as an Augustinian monastery in either 1140 or 1148. The elder Lady Chapel off the north transept was added in about 1220-80 and also survives. The four bayed choir, its aisles and the eastern Lady Chapel were rebuilt between c1298-1340 whilst the transepts and central tower built 1473-c1515 were delayed probably because of the cathedral's lack of finances. The church became a cathedral in 1542 following the closure of its monastery in December 1539. Work on rebuilding the nave started in 1543 but was stopped almost immediately, again because of money problems. The church fell into disrepair, losing its cathedral status to Gloucester in 1836. Work on the nave and west front recommenced between 1868-88 under architect George Edmund Street whilst J.L. Pearson undertook restoration work from 1888-1905. Bristol regained its outright cathedral status in 1897.

75. Bury St Edmunds Abbey (Cathedral status 1914-present, built 1510-30, extended 1865-1965). Bury St. Edmunds was one of East Anglia's most important towns with its church, founded around 633, becoming a pilgrimage site following the acquisition in 903 of the remains of King Edmund, who had been murdered by the Vikings in 869. It became a Benedictine monastery in 1020 and, when it was decided to move the East Anglian bishopric from Thetford in 1094, it was believed the original intention was to move it to Bury St Edmunds but an early episcopal charter preventing this could not be overturned. The church was rebuilt by the Normans from about 1090 which took about a century to complete. The settlement was fortified in the 14th Century following rioting by the local inhabitants and by the time it was dissolved in 1539, it was one of the country's wealthiest possessing a large, outstanding abbey church. Following its closure, the monastery was pillaged with only fragments of its former glory and size visible today. One of the two parish churches in its precincts, St James, mostly built from 1510-30 by master mason John Wastell, was made into the cathedral of St Edmundsbury in 1914. The nave roof and chancel were rebuilt in 1711, the latter being rebuilt by Sir George Gilbert Scott in 1865-9. Further enlargements to the cathedral were undertaken in the 1960's involving a new crossing, choir, chapter rooms and chapels by architect S.D. Bower. Later additions include a new choir school, visitors centre, works to the cloisters, north transept and a new central tower built 2000-10 to a design by Hugh Mathew. Today the remains of the monastery, its impressive 12th Century gatehouse and the other parish church are open to the public.

02. Canterbury Cathedral (Cathedral status c602-present, crypt built 1096-1185, above ground mainly built 1175-1505). The cathedral is the seat of the Archbishop of Canterbury who is the religious leader of the Church of England and the worldwide Anglican Communion. Its importance has resulted in the cathedral undergoing numerous building and alteration projects frequently being the pioneer of new design ideas. Canterbury has been inhabited since the Iron Age and became an important centre for both the Romans and the Jutes, who settled here from north Europe from the 5th Century. No remains have been found of the Roman church described by Bede which was repaired by St Augustine in c598-c602 and is thought to lie beneath the current cathedral. A total or partial replacement church was built in the 10th Century before a Benedictine monastery supporting up to 150 monks was added in c997. Damage caused by Danish raiders in 1011 necessitated some restoration works between 1042-50 before a fire destroyed this cathedral in 1067. Following the appointment of the first Norman archbishop Lanfranc, the church was completely rebuilt between 1071-7 similar in style to the one found at Caen in France. It was cruciform in shape, some 95 metres in length, with a nine-bay nave, transepts with apsidal chapels, short choir with a semi-circular apse, a central tower and two further west ones. Only fragments of masonry from this church survive in current transepts. Within 20 years of completion, it was decided to extend the east end to accommodate more conveniently processions and pilgrims which was undertaken between 1096-1126. Little remains of this work except the western half of the crypt which was completed in c1105. Another fire destroyed the east end necessitating masons William of Sens and William the Englishman to rebuild and extend it between 1175-85 to cater for the increased number of pilgrims visiting the shrine of Archbishop Thomas Becket who was infamously murdered in the north transept in 1170. This work remains largely intact as does the enlarged crypt. Two hundred years elapsed before the next substantial building project. A new nave to match the eastern arm was long overdue and this was done along with the rebuilding of the main transepts, the cloisters and strengthening the crossing piers between 1379 and 1414 by the royal master mason Henry Yeveley. The body of King Henry IV was interned here in 1413 to join other notable religious figures like Lanfranc and Theodore. The chapter house and the western towers were completed 1400-34 by Stephen Lote and Thomas Mapilton whilst the north transept and adjoining Lady Chapel date from 1448-55 by Richard Beke. The 78 metre tall central tower, known as the Bell Harry tower, was erected between about 1468-1505 by John Wassell, who was also responsible for the Great Gatehouse erected c1515-20. The monastery was dissolved in 1540, being made a secular 'New Foundation' cathedral in April 1541. It has undergone major restoration works in the 19th and 20th centuries by George Austin and W.D. Caröe, who replaced and repaired the cathedral's towers. The remains of the monastery are the best preserved and largest of any English cathedral.

42. Carlisle Cathedral (Cathedral status 1133-present, built c1125-1419, 19th Century restorations). Carlisle was established by the Romans to serve the forts protecting Hadrian's Wall which then separated Scotland from England. A church for secular canons was set up in 1102 just ten years after Carlisle was taken from the Scots, becoming an Augustinian priory for regular canons in c1123. The church was largely completed before it became a cathedral in 1133 with only two bays of the nave and part of the south transept surviving from this period. The choir, aisles and arcading dating from 1245 were destroyed by fires in 1292, 1316 and 1363 and were rebuilt in their present form from 1293-1395, probably by Ivo de Raghton and John Lewyn. The north transept, central tower and choir stalls date from 1400-19. The monastery was dissolved in 1540 and was re-established with secular clergy in May 1541. Six of the eight nave bays were demolished and the materials were used to reinforce the nearby castle during the English Civil Wars. The cathedral underwent restoration in the 19th Century principally between 1853-70 by Ewan Christian and in the following century by S.E. Dykes Bower and others. There are the remains of some monastery buildings including the cloister and refectory.

76. Chelmsford Cathedral (Cathedral status 1914-present, built 1424-1803, extended 1873-1926). The original church probably dates from the 12th Century when a market town was founded next to a bridge crossing the River Can with fragments of this Norman church being found in the present tower. In 1424 the church was rebuilt with the current choir, the western tower and the south porch dating from this period. The nave was restored following a collapse in 1801-3 by John Johnson and in 1873 a northern aisle to the nave and a transept were added. The former parish church of St Mary the Virgin became a cathedral with the formation of England's second most populated diocese in 1914. The eastern end was extended with the chapter house and vestries being added to the north side in 1923-6 by Sir Charles Nicholson.

46. Chester Cathedral (Cathedral status 1541-present, mainly built 1093-1537 with some 19th Century restorations). Chester was founded by the Romans in 79AD and became one of their three main military bases. The current cathedral site was probably used for a Roman religious basilica, an Anglo-Saxon convent and a 10th Century church for secular canons, with excavations discovering fragments of this later structure. This church was demolished in 1090 to make way for the Benedictine monastery of St. Werburgh. The abbey church was constructed from 1093 to 1140 with the surviving north transept, parts of the nave and the north-west tower dating from this period. Work was delayed by a nave fire in 1114. The choir was twice rebuilt from 1194, the surviving one by Richard Lenginour dates from c1283-1315, along with a chapter house (c1230-50) and the Lady Chapel (1265-90) which was built with no foundations. Parts of the nave and the massive south transept were built 1323-49 by Nicholas de Derneford requiring an adjoining parish church to be demolished to make way for it with its parochial function being incorporated into the new transept. The Black Death and lack of money meant that the nave was not completed until 1492 probably by William Rediche, while the south transept, central and south-west towers, porch, west front and cloisters date from 1493-1537 possibly by Seth and George Derwall. The church became a cathedral for the Bishop of Chester in 1541 after the monastery was closed in 1539. The cathedral has since been subjected to a series of major and controversial restoration works involving Thomas Harrison (1818-20), Richard Charles Hussey (1843-64), Sir George Gilbert Scott (1868-76), Sir Arthur William and Charles James Blomfield (1882-1902) which have added further confusion to the already complex medieval fabric of the church. The free-standing bell tower is by George Pace and was erected from 1973-5.

35. Chichester Cathedral (Cathedral status 1075-present, mainly built 1075-1402, towers rebuilt in the 19th Century). Dating from Roman times, the current cathedral site previously accommodated an Anglo-Saxon church founded in 681 of which no remains have been discovered. Chichester's cathedral was started in 1075 after the bishop's seat was moved from Selsey with the presbytery being consecrated in 1108. A fire in 1114 disrupted construction with work to the nave and tower not being complete until about 1148. The apsidal east end with radiating chapels were replaced by a two-bay square retro-choir between 1187-99 probably by Walter of Coventry following another fire. The central and heightened south-west towers, additional chapels and the west porch date from 1215-75 whilst the two-bay extension to the Lady Chapel and remodelled south transept are from 1288-1337. John the Mason completed the spire in 1402, Walter Walton the free standing campanile in 1440 to house the cathedral's bells and possibly William Wynford the cloisters in 1500. The spire collapsed in 1861 and was rebuilt along with the central tower by Sir George Gilbert Scott (1861-6) whilst J.L. Pearson replaced the north-west tower in 1899-1901. Structural repairs to the cathedral were undertaken in the 1960's.

79. Coventry Cathedral (Cathedral status 1918-present, built 1956-62). Coventry is an ancient settlement dating back to the Iron Age, continuing through Roman and Anglo-Saxon times. It expanded during the Industrial Revolution thanks to watchmaking, car and bicycle manufacturing. The current cathedral is the city's third. St. Michael's church, on a different site from the first Coventry cathedral known as St Mary's Priory which was destroyed during the Reformation, served as a parish church being built mainly between 1378 and the early 16th Century. In 1918 it became a cathedral for the newly formed diocese but was badly damaged in 1940 by German fire bombs during World War II. Its remains, the tower, 90 metre tall spire and outer walls, stand next to the current cathedral as a poignant reminder of the conflict. Sir Giles Gilbert Scott produced an imaginative design to incorporate much of the damaged church into a massive new rebuild but this scheme never materialised. Instead the third Coventry cathedral was built 1956-62 to a design by Basil Spence after he successfully won an international architectural competition involving over 200 entrants. It was the fourth new Anglican cathedral built, cost in the region of £985,000 (PDV £24.1 million) and is a modern version of a church hall entered by an open portico from the ruins of the former cathedral.

84. Derby Cathedral (Cathedral status 1927-present, built 1511-30, 1723-5 and 1965-72). Even though Derby has a history dating back to Roman and Anglo-Saxon times, it was the coming of the railways and specialist manufacturing in the 19th Century that increased its size and importance. Nothing remains of the original church built on the current site or indeed the cathedral's immediate predecessor which was roughly the same size. The present church dates from the mid-14th Century although only its dominating 65 metre tower added between 1511-30 survives. It had a resident college consisting of a dean and seven priests at this time before being dissolved in 1549 with its independent 'Royal Peculiar' title (see Westminster Abbey) persisting into the 19th Century. In 1723 the church was in such a poor state of repair that a cleric employed a gang of labourers who demolished it in a single night except for the tower! It was substantially rebuilt in 1723-5 in a Renaissance style by architect James

Gibbs with enlargements to the east end involving retro-choir and a series of rooms undertaken 1965-72 by architect Sebastian Comper. The former All Saints' parish church was granted cathedral status in 1927.

31. Durham Cathedral (Cathedral status 995-present, mainly built 1093-1280, some later additions and restorations). The history of the cathedral dates from around 995 when displaced Celtic monks from Lindisfarne chose a strategic and dramatic site overlooking the river Wear at Durham to build a new monastery to house the relics of St Cuthbert, their revered former bishop. A temporary church, probably built of timber, was used until a more permanent stone one was consecrated in 998. After the 1066 Norman Conquest, King William appointed a fellow countryman William of Carilef as bishop which resulted in the rebuilding of the cathedral on a grand scale served from 1083 by an attached Benedictine monastery of 23 monks. Building works commenced in 1093 with the choir being completed in 1099 and the nave in 1133, the greater part of which stands today with the exception of the east end. A chapter house were added 1133-40 and the western Galilee chapel c1170-75 by Richard Wolveston housed the remains of the Venerable Bede. The west towers were finished in around 1220 while Richard Farnham build the 'Chapel of Nine Altars' at the east end between 1242-80. The cloisters were constructed 1390-1418 by John Lewyn and Thomas Mapilton while the central tower, damaged by lightning in 1429, was replaced and heightened in 1465-90 possibly by Thomas Barton and John Bell jnr. The monastery was dissolved in 1539 and a secular chapter was established to run the cathedral in May 1541. The cathedral was used by Oliver Cromwell to house Scottish prisoners-of-war taken during the Civil Wars which resulted in over 1,500 deaths and extensive damage to the church's fabric. Some controversial demolitions and changes were undertaken by the infamous James Wyatt between 1795-7 whilst the chapter house was later restored by Hodgson Fowler in 1895. The central tower and cloisters were refurbished in the 20th Century. Today Durham is the finest and least altered example of a Norman cathedral in England and possesses extensive converted monastic outbuildings.

41. Ely Cathedral (Cathedral status 1109-present, mainly built 1090-c1400, various later additions and restorations). Ely was built on an island in the Fens, the marshy region in Eastern England which was not fully drained until the 17th Century. The first monastery for nuns was established by Etheldreda, daughter of the King of East Anglia, in 673. It was believed that this settlement was destroyed by Viking raiders in the late 9th Century but between 963 and 969 a Benedictine monastery was established for up to 70 monks as part of Dunstan's monastic revival. The current cathedral dates from 1083 when the first Norman abbot instructed the demolition of the previous abbey church. Work started on the east end with the choir and central tower being completed in 1106, both since demolished. The surviving north and south transepts, west transepts, apses and tower and the 69 metre long 13-bay nave (reduced by one by the subsequent building of the octagon) date from c1090-1197. Ely become a cathedral in 1109, formed out of Lincoln's massive diocese. Work continued with the building of a west Galilee porch in c1200 and from c1235-52 the east end was extended with a six-bay 33 metre long presbytery by mason Sampson. This retro-choir, which cost £5,040.93 (PDV £4.3 million), was paid by bishop Northwold and the shrine of St Ethelreda was dedicated in the presence of Henry III on 15 October 1252. Work started on the free-standing Lady Chapel in 1321 which was finished in 1349. At over 15 metres in width, it is the largest span stone-vaulted building found in any English medieval church. In February 1322 the central tower collapsed and was replaced by the unique octagon lantern which provides light to the central crossing. Constructed from oak, probably by master carpenter William Hurley with the eight massive supporting piers by masons John of Ramsey and John Atte Grene, it was completed by 1340 at a cost of £2,046.35 (£1.63 million). From c1395 a lantern was added to the western tower to match the central one by Robert Wodehirst and the Great Gatehouse (1396-1400) was erected by John Meppushal. Since this date various other elements, the stalls, two chantry chapels to honour bishops Alcock and West, part of cloisters were added before the monastery was closed in 1539 and re-reformed under secular clergy in September 1541. The cathedral suffered damage to its fixtures and fittings during this process and has since undergone some large scale restoration work most notably by the controversial architect James Essex (1757-62) and Sir George Gilbert Scott from 1847. There are the remains of some monastery buildings, now largely converted to other uses.

32. Exeter Cathedral (Cathedral status 1050-present, mainly built from 1112 and 1275-1382, additions 1413-1519). Exeter, built on a ridge overlooking a navigable river, predates the Romans who founded a city here in the 1st Century which the Anglo-Saxons continued to occupy. The seat of the Bishop of Devon and Cornwall was transferred to Exeter from Crediton in 1050 probably because it was more easily defendable. Nothing remains of an earlier Anglo-Saxon Benedictine abbey that occupied the site but following the Conquest a new Norman bishop was appointed and he finally set about rebuilding the cathedral on a grander, Continental style in the 12th Century. Construction work probably commenced in 1112 on the east end, transepts with towers over but by late 13th Century the building was already deemed to be out of date. Only the two transept towers and, less significantly, the lower parts of the aisle walls survived the subsequent rebuilding. The church was rebuilt in the Gothic Decorative style starting in around 1275 with the Lady Chapel, square retro-choir and presbytery by Roger the Mason completed in 1308 with Bishop Walter de Stapledon contributing £1,800 (£1.49 million) towards the cost. Exeter is unique for an English cathedral in having no central crossing tower. The crossing and eastern part of the nave by William Luve was finished by 1328 whilst the since demolished cloisters and the rest of the nave including the west front were completed between 1323-82 by Thomas Witney, Richard Farleigh and Robert Lesyngham. Like nearby Wells, the west façade contains figures of saints, apostles, angels and kings of Wessex and England. The 13th Century chapter house was rebuilt from its foundations by John Tynlegh and John Harry between 1413-39 whilst Oldham and Speke chantry chapels were added in 1504-19. Damage to the cathedral occurred following the Reformation and during the English Civil Wars, when the cloisters were destroyed. Refurbishment works were undertaken during the Victorian era by Sir George Gilbert Scott (1870-7) and J.L. Pearson (1887). A bomb destroyed a chapel and a section of wall during the Second World War. Exeter possesses some of this country's finest cathedral choir fittings including the oldest bishop's throne, most extensive misericords, sedilia and pulpitum.

47. Gloucester Cathedral (Cathedral status 1541-present, mainly built 1089-1160, 1318-74 and 1421-83). Gloucester was founded in 97AD by the Romans on level ground next to the river Severn. The first monastery for monks and nuns dates from about 681, becoming a house for secular priests in 823 and a Benedictine monastery in c1022. The abbey was rebuilt in 1058 following a fire but when the last Anglo-Saxon abbot died in 1072 the monastery had just two monks and eight novices. Sero, his successor, commenced a major rebuild in 1089 which forms the basis of the present cathedral. The crypt, choir and nave were finished by 1100 although fires in 1102 and 1120 delayed the nave's completion until 1160. The since demolished central tower dates from 1222 whilst the nave vaulting, probably by John of Gloucester, is from 1242-45. The body of King Edward II was interned here in 1327 following his murder at Berkeley Castle which brought increased wealth to the abbey. This new money enabled further building work which included the south aisle of the nave, north and south transepts and the choir from 1318-74 by Martin of Sponebed and William of Ramsey. This started a trend in England with the Norman fabric being stripped back and having a Perpendicular Gothic veneer applied. The giant east window measuring 21 by nearly 13 metres is the largest found in an English medieval cathedral. The surviving, distinct fan-vaulted cloisters dates from c1370-1412 are by Robert Lesyngham whilst from 1421-83 the west front, two nave bays, the south porch, the 75 metre high central tower and the Lady

Chapel were added, the last two by John Hobbs. The monastery was shut down in 1540 and it became a cathedral in 1541 when a see was created out of neighbouring Worcester. Gloucester briefly took over the Bristol see from 1836-97 while the cathedral has undergone extensive restoration works involving F.S. Waller from 1847 and Sir George Gilbert Scott six years later.

85. Guildford Cathedral (Cathedral status 1927-present, built 1936-1961). Guildford dates from Anglo-Saxon times and developed in a gap in the North Downs next to the river Wey. The diocese was created in 1927 out of the Winchester see and Holy Trinity church, in the centre of the town, became a temporary or pro-Cathedral. This church dates from 1763 when it replaced an earlier church which was destroyed when its steeple collapsed. A new cathedral, on a different site known as Stag Hill, was designed by architectural competition winner Sir Edward Maufe and was begun in 1936. The Second World War interrupted progress meaning it was not consecrated until 1961 although the crypt was open for services from 1947. It therefore became the third new Anglican cathedral to be completed in England since the Reformation.

16. Hereford Cathedral (Cathedral status c679-present, mainly built 1079-1260, c1325-70 and c1470-1530). Hereford was founded as an Anglo-Saxon military base next to a ford on the river Wye. It has been the seat of a bishop since c679 when the original church was replaced by a more substantial one following the burial of Ethelbert, king of East Anglia, who was murdered nearby in 794. His relics attracted substantial numbers of pilgrims. The church underwent extensive alterations in the 11th Century before being badly damaged and plundered by a Welsh raid in 1056. It was rebuilt following the Norman Conquest from 1079 until around 1145 with the nave, choir and parts of the transepts of this church surviving in the current cathedral. Between 1190-1260, the east end with its three apses was replaced by a 17 metre long Lady Chapel with crypt below, eastern transepts were built and chantry chapels were added to the northern transept. The precarious state of the central tower and the south-east transept meant that they had to be rebuilt from c1325-70. Only fragments remain of the ten-sided chapter house built 1359-70 by John of Evesham and Thomas of Cambridge while the bishop's cloisters were commenced 1412-8 by Thomas Denyar. Two further chantry chapels for Bishops Audley and Stanbury, the north porch and the completion of the bishop's and vicars' cloisters date from c1470-1530. The cathedral suffered severe damage during the English Civil Wars when Hereford changed hands on several occasions. In 1786 the west tower collapsed causing extensive damage to the west end and part of the nave. Restoration work was undertaken by the notorious James Wyatt (1786-96) with subsequent alterations and renovation works by L.N. and N.J. Cottingham

(1841-52) and to the west front by J. Oldrid Scott (1902-8). There are remains of the adjacent monastic buildings whilst the cathedral houses the famous 'Mappa Mundi', a 13th Century religious map of the World and has the country's only surviving 'chained' library.

86. Leicester Cathedral (Cathedral status 1927-present, west of the central crossing built 12th-15th centuries, east 1847-1927). Leicester was established as a military settlement by the Romans in around AD50 on Fosse Way, a main road linking Exeter and Lincoln and developed into an important trading town. This increased during the 18th Century when it became a centre for engineering, shoemaking and hosiery. The present cathedral was chosen from five existing parish churches when the new diocese of Leicester was re-established in 1926 with St. Martin church becoming a cathedral in the following year. Only fragments of masonry remain from the aisle-less, cruciform shaped Norman church with aisles and chapels being added in the 13th Century and the west end in the 15th. The 73 metre tall central tower and spire, transepts, clerestory and chancel chapels were rebuilt by Raphael Brandon in 1847-67 with later additions and restorations being undertaken by J.L. Pearson, G.E. Street and Sir Charles Nicholson between 1896 and 1927. This means that virtually everything east of the tower is Victorian and later. The only addition since the church was given cathedral status in 1927 is the vestry block added by William Keay in 1938/9. In 2012 the remains of King Richard III were discovered in a car park close to the cathedral. He was killed in 1485 at nearby Bosworth Fields, the decisive battle of the War of the Roses fought between the houses of Lancaster and York, and his remains were interned in the cathedral in 2015.

14. Lichfield Cathedral (Cathedral status 669-1075; (c1143?-1248?) & 1248-present, mainly built 1195-c1385). A fortress was established by the Romans in the Lichfield area as it was near the crossing of Icknield and Watling Streets, two of their great roads crossing the country. In 669 Bishop Chad moved the see of Mercia in the Midlands to Lichfield, possibly from Repton, and the church of St Mary become a cathedral. A replacement church was built in 700 to house the remains of the now enshrined St Chad which attracted large numbers of pilgrims. Excavations have found evidence of both these Anglo-Saxon churches beneath the current cathedral. As the town was not walled and therefore susceptible to attack, the see was moved to the more secure and significant town of Chester in 1075 and onto Coventry in 1102. Surprisingly this did not prevent a large Norman replacement church being started in 1085, fragments of which have been discovered below ground. A civil war and a major dispute between the monks at Coventry and the secular clerics at Lichfield meant that between around 1143 and 1248 it was uncertain which of the two cities hosted the cathedral. The argument was resolved with a joint ownership agreement which lasted until 1539 when it returned solely to Lichfield. The building of the current cathedral dates from 1195 with only piers and arches of the three west bays of the choir and the sacristy to the south side still standing from this period. For the next 130 years from c1220, the cathedral was largely rebuilt: transepts, chapter house and vestibule in 1249 by mason Thomas; nave, west front, central tower and west spires in 1320 probably by William FitzThomas, Thomas Wallace, Nicholas and William of Eyton. The Lady Chapel and east end date from 1350 and are attributed to William of Eyton and William of Ramsey, the king's mason. It is thought the unique surviving three spires were completed by Gilbert the Mason in around 1385. The cathedral suffered extensive damage caused by the Reformation, a plague, a spire collapse and the English Civil Wars, all of which left the cathedral in an abject state of repair. Major restoration work was undertaken by Sir William Wilson between 1661-9, the controversial James Wyatt in 1788-90 and by Sir George Gilbert Scott and his son, J.O. Scott from 1856-84.

33. Lincoln Cathedral (Cathedral status c1075-present, built, altered and extended 1074-c1548). Dating from the Iron Age, Lincoln became an important Roman fortress and trading town being located next to the navigable river Witham and at the northern end of Fosse Way, one of their main roads. The first Norman bishop following the Conquest moved the bishopric to Lincoln from the isolated small town of Dorchester-on-Thames in around 1075. Work started on building a 103 metre long new cathedral in 1074 on the current prominent site overlooking the city and was consecrated in 1092, only parts of the west front and western tower survive. An 1141 arson attack during the Battle of Lincoln and an earthquake cum tower collapse in 1185 caused extensive damage. A large rebuilding programme in the new Gothic style followed starting with the choir and east transept (1192-1210) possibly by Geoffrey de Noyers from Northamptonshire and Richard the Mason. The main transepts followed in c1215-30 by Michael the Mason, the 21 metre diameter, ten-sided chapter house (c1220-35), nave, the massive west front and the lower part of the central tower (c1225-55) following another collapse in 1239 are all by master mason Alexander. The east end was extended by five-bays beyond the eastern transepts (now known as the Angel Choir) similar to Ely from 1256-80 by Simon of Thirsk. The cloisters (1295-1310) probably by Richard of Stow were originally built with no foundations. It was hardly surprising that they soon showed signs of distress and had to be rebuilt. The surviving central tower was heightened between 1307-11 by Richard of Stow to 69 metres to become the highest of any English cathedral, paid for by the granting of indulgencies to wealthy deviants. Even more dramatic was the addition of a 175 metre tall spire which was reputed to be the tallest structure in the world at the time until it collapsed in 1549, never to be replaced. The glorious stalls depict eleven of England's kings from William I to Edward III date from c1363-72. The west towers were raised to 75 metres maybe by mason Geoffrey in c1400, originally with timber spires which were removed in 1807, with three chantry chapels' added between c1475-c1548. Sir Christopher Wren rebuilt part of the cloisters in 1680 whilst the infamous James Essex (1762-5) and R.S. Godfrey (1922-32) undertook extensive later restoration works. The cathedral possesses one of the four surviving copies of the Magna Carta.

68. Liverpool Cathedral (Cathedral status 1880-present, built 1904-78). Liverpool expanded enormously in the 18th Century with the opening of the docks that serviced the rapid industrial growth of Lancashire in north-west England. The diocese was founded in 1880 to reflect this increase and the parish church of St. Peters (built 1699-1704) was used as a temporary or pro-cathedral before being demolished in 1923. An earlier scheme to build a new cathedral was abandoned before 22 year old Giles Gilbert Scott won a competition in 1903 to design it on a dominant site in the city centre overlooking the river Mersey. Site restrictions meant that the church had to be built on an unusual north-south axis parallel to the river with the Lady Chapel being the first part to be opened in 1910. The First World War held up work but in 1924 the chancel, ambulatory, chapter house and vestries were consecrated. Further delays and World War Two meant the cathedral was not fully complete and opened until 1978, 18 years after Scott's death. It was therefore the fifth and last new build Anglican cathedral completed in this country. Like Sir Christopher Wren's work at St Pauls, Scott constantly revised his original design, frequently rebuilding completed works which not surprisingly resulted in a lengthy, budget-breaking construction period. His cathedral is full of superlatives: at 188.7 metres in length it is the longest cathedral in the world as St Peter's in Rome at 211.5 metres is strictly speaking a basilica not a cathedral; it is the seventh largest church in the world whilst its bells are the highest, at 67 metres, and, at 16.5 tons, the heaviest.

04. London - St Paul's Cathedral (Cathedral status 604-616; 675-present, built 1675-1710). London dates from the Bronze Age but it was the Romans who founded the first significant settlement in 43AD and by the 2nd Century it had a population of 60,000, superseding Colchester as the country's capital. Its fortunes declined during the Anglo-Saxon period being replaced in importance by Winchester but on the eve of the Norman Conquest it was once again the largest and most important city in the kingdom. The current St Paul's Cathedral is either the fourth or fifth one to occupy the site, the highest point in the City of London. A bishop of London attended a meeting as early as 314 but the location of his Roman cathedral is unknown. Augustine's missionaries set up England's third episcopal see here in 604 and a cathedral was built, probably on or close to the current site. The bishop was expelled from London in around 616 and was forced to set up a base in a former Roman fort in Essex (see Bradwell-on-Sea) until the diocese was re-established in the capital in 675. The fate of the first cathedral is not known but it was either rebuilt or replaced around this time. Fire destroyed this church in 962 and its successor in 1087. The Normans built the third or fourth cathedral, known as Old St Paul's, starting in around 1090 at the east end. Work to the nave commenced in about 1110 possibly by Andrew the Mason before yet another fire required further remediation, including to the tower, from 1137 to 1221. A major rebuild started in 1251 at the east end possibly by Michael of Canterbury and John Weldon and was completed in 1321 involving the transepts, a chapter house and the cloisters by William of Ramsey while Henry Yeveley installed various fixtures from 1374-c1390. When complete it was the finest cathedral in England with its overall length at over 214 metres meant it was the longest church every built in the world and its spire at 170 metres the second tallest after Lincoln's. In 1561 a lightning strike destroyed the spire and it was never replaced. The cathedral suffered severe damage during the Reformation and neglect thereafter which required architect Inigo Jones to carry out some controversial restoration works from 1631-40. Old St Paul's was finally destroyed by the Great Fire of London in 1666 and a decision was taken to rebuild it anew, funded from a tax on coal imported into the capital. Sir Christopher Wren was commissioned to design it, overseeing its construction along with 50 other ruined City churches, an unprecedented achievement. He was paid £200 per year (£28,400) and was assisted by master masons Joshua Marshall and Edward Strong. The design went through a number of modifications, one of which can be viewed today in the cathedral, the great timber model of 1673. Building work commenced on 21st June 1675, with the old cathedral finally being fully demolished in 1686. The new cathedral was consecrated in 1697, deemed fully complete by 1710 just 35 years after the first foundation stone was laid at a cost of £736,752 (£101 million). It was England's first new cathedral erected since the Reformation, being built in a Renaissance style and designed for Protestant worship. Cruciform in shape, it is 170 metres in length with its crypt below serving as a mausoleum for many famous Englishmen, including Wren himself. The famous dome with its ball and cross terminating 122 metres above ground level was the capital's tallest structure until as recently as 1962. The cathedral survived three direct bomb attacks during the Second World War and a contemporary photograph taken during a raid became one of the iconic images of the war.

73. London - Southwark Cathedral (Cathedral status 1905-present), built 1213-1395, 1510-20 and 1889-97). Southwark cathedral is built on the site of St Mary Overie Augustinian Priory for regular canons, which operated from 1106 until it was dissolved in 1539 when it became a parish church. The site was used for religious worship even before this dating back to 852. Building of the present church started in around 1213 following a fire with only fragments of the Norman church surviving in the north transept and north nave aisle. The choir and retro-choir were completed in 1235 possibly by Richard the Mason, and today survives all be it much restored. The transepts and since demolished nave were started in c1273 while Henry Yeveley constructed the lower part of the central tower, the west front (since rebuilt) and restored the fire damaged south transept in the late 14th Century. The tower was heightened in 1510-20 possibly by Thomas Berty. The church underwent extensive Victorian restoration work in 1822-35 by George Gwilt whilst the unstable nave was rebuilt, including the west end, by Sir Arthur Blomfield between 1889-97. In 1905 the diocese of Southwark was created out of the Rochester and Winchester sees and the former parish church of St. Saviour was given cathedral status.

52. Manchester Cathedral (Cathedral status 1847-present, built 1422-1520, 1862-present). The Romans drove out the native Britons from the area and built a fort here in the 1st Century AD. Manchester expanded enormously during the Industrial Revolution being the centre for textile manufacturing thanks to the arrival of navigable canals and the railways. The current cathedral site was home to an early Saxon church and a parish church after the lord of the manor, Robert Greslet, donated land next to his manor house in 1215. After becoming a collegiate church in 1421, the church was demolished in 1422 and rebuilt afresh. The choir was finished in 1450, the nave in 1480 with chantry chapels being added some 40 years later to both the north and south sides of the church making it after St Michael's of Coventry the second widest English parish church. The priory was closed in 1547 with most of its collegiate buildings surviving in the adjacent school of music. An outer south chapel was added and the tower was heightened in 1862-8 by J.P. Holden. The church underwent extensive 19th and 20th Century restoration and rebuilding work following its status change to become a cathedral in 1847 when the diocese of Manchester was created. This included rebuilding the north and south porches, repairing the war damaged Lady Chapel and new vestries, library and north chapel.

69. Newcastle Cathedral (Cathedral status 1882-present, 1359-1448, substantial later alterations and additions). The Romans created the first recorded settlement in the 2nd Century AD, building a fort and crossing over the river Tyne. The town expanded during the Industrial Revolution becoming a centre for ship building and heavy engineering. The cathedral was originally the parish church of St. Nicholas, which dates from the 11th Century. The Norman church suffered two fires in the 13th Century with only masonry fragments surviving. The nave and transepts were built after 1359 while the tower dates from c1410 and the highly visible lantern spire was added in 1448. It was rebuilt in the late 19th Century by Sir George Gilbert Scott. The church suffered damage caused by Scottish invasions in 1640 and 1644, vandalism between 1783-7 whilst the library, porches and vestries were added in 1736, 1834 and 1926 respectively. The eastern end was remodelled and fitted out by R.J. Johnson when it became a cathedral in 1882, created out of the diocese of Durham.

38. Norwich Cathedral (Cathedral status c1094-present, mainly built 1096-1145, some later additions). The Romans made nearby Caistor the capital of East Anglia following their defeat of the local Iceni tribe led by Boudicca. Norwich became one of England's wealthiest cities during the Middle Ages, the direct result of the wool trade. The Normans moved rural sees to more easily defendable urban ones so once the prior of Fecamp abbey Normandy, Herbert de Losinga, brought the East Anglian bishopric for £1,900 (PDV £1.7 million) he transferred the bishop's seat from Thetford to Norwich in around 1094. Parts of a Saxon settlement incorporating two churches were demolished in 1096 to make way for the cathedral and its accompanying Benedictine monastery served by 60 monks. The cathedral was completed in 1145 with the 14-bay 84 metre long nave, transepts, east end with apsidal chapels (except for windows and vaulting) surviving in the current building. This was mainly due to the cathedral having no shrine, meaning that the eastern arm did not require extending. Originally a smaller spire capped the tower, being completed in about 1170. A since demolished chapter house was built 1289-1303 whilst the cloisters were added between 1297-1430 by John and William of Ramsey and Robert and James Woderofe. The timber spire was blown down in 1362 and its replacement was struck by lightning in 1463. It was rebuilt in stone between 1464-72 by Robert Everard and at 96 metres in height is England's second tallest surviving spire after Salisbury. The presbytery clerestory was added c1362-9 by Robert Wodehirst while James Woderofe rebuilt the west front 1426-50 and nave, presbytery and transept ceiling vaulting were undertaken between c1464-1536 mostly by Robert Everard. The cathedral was the first to be reconfigured as a secular 'New Foundation' one immediately after the monastery was dissolved in May 1538. Restoration work was carried out by Anthony Salvin and Edward Blore in 1830-40 and St. Saviour's war memorial chapel replaced the Lady Chapel at the east end in 1930-2 by Sir Charles Nicholson. The cloisters survived the Reformation but the other monastic buildings were either demolished or converted for other uses.

51. Oxford Cathedral (Cathedral status 1546-present, built 1158-80, 1220-1355 and 1525-9). Oxford adjoined a crossing of the river Thames and developed around England's oldest university which was founded in the 12th Century. A nunnery was established in around 727 before becoming the Augustinian priory of St. Frideswide in 1122 for regular canons. Five bays of the nave, the choir, transepts and the lower part of central tower all built 1158-80 survive although the rest of the old priory church was demolished. Between 1220-50, the tower was heightened and a spire added, with a free-standing chapter house and a Lady Chapel built in the outer aisle on the north side of the choir. To this was added the Latin Chapel in c1350-5 and the cloisters from 1478-1503 probably by William Orchard. After the priory was dissolved in 1524 it become Cardinal Wolsey's college, later Christ Church College. As part of this process four bays of the nave were demolished to make way for the great quadrangle which along with a hall were undertaken by John Lebons and Henry Redman between 1525-9. The church became both the chapel for the college and, from 1546, the cathedral for the diocese of Oxford, replacing nearby Osney. Restoration work was undertaken in the 19th Century by Sir George Gilbert Scott whilst the western porch was added in 1872/3 by G.F. Bodley.

48. Peterborough Cathedral (Cathedral status 1541-present, built 1118-1230, 1335-75 and c1496-1508). One of the first monasteries in Anglo-Saxon Mercia was established in Medeshamstede (Peterborough), a quiet backwater next to the river Nene, in around 655. The monastery survived until the Vikings destroyed it in 870 but the Benedictine revival in c970 resulted in extensions to both the monastic buildings and to the Anglo-Saxon church, the remains of which have been uncovered beneath the south transept of the current cathedral. In 1116 a fire allegedly started in the monks kitchen severely damaged the abbey church which resulted in the rebuilding on a much larger, Norman style commencing in 1118. The limestone came from a local quarry at Barnack which the monastery owned and is today a nature reserve, open to the public. The east end and transepts were complete by 1155 and the nine-bay nave by 1175. By 1193 the nave was extended by two-bays in a different architectural style and west towers with shallow transepts added. The unrivalled three arched west front was built between 1193-1230 so the current structure was essentially complete by this date and is therefore the last surviving great Norman cathedral in England. The unique timber nave roof can still be seen and dates from around 1230-50. The first phase of the cloisters were constructed in c1220-60 with the since demolished Lady Chapel being attached to the north transept in 1272-90. The Black Death had a devastating impact on the monastery reducing the number of monks from 64 to just 32. The central tower dates from around 1335, the two-storeyed Galilee porch in the central west end arch is from around 1375 whilst the cloisters were finished in about 1475. The rectangular east end extension still known as the 'New Building' was added c1496-1508 with a fan-vaulted ceiling probably by John Wastell, who was responsible for a similar one at nearby King's College, Cambridge. The monastery was dissolved in 1539 and became the cathedral for the new diocese of Peterborough formed out of Lincoln two years later. Catherine of Aragon, first wife of Henry VIII and a central figure in the Reformation, is buried here. Mary, Queen of Scots was briefly interned in the cathedral following her execution at nearby Fotheringhay Castle in 1587 before her remains were moved to Westminster Abbey. The cathedral suffered severe damage during the English Civil Wars with fittings and fixture destroyed, the cloisters wrecked and the Lady Chapel completely demolished. The church underwent extensive Victorian restoration under Edward Blore (1827-32) while J.L. Pearson rebuilt the central tower. Fragments of the monasteries cloisters, refectory, infirmary and dormitory can still be seen.

87. Portsmouth Cathedral (Cathedral status 1927-present, built in late 12th Century, 1683-93 and 1935-1991). The origins of Portsmouth are disputed with Saxons and Normans both laying claim to founding the first port which developed into a major naval base giving the town its notoriety and wealth. An Augustinian chapel was established here in around 1188 with only the choir arm and transepts surviving. This chapel was extended, eventually becoming a parish church and finally a cathedral. The old central tower has an interesting history being used as a lighthouse and as a look-out during the misnamed 'One-hundred Year War' with France. The Royal forces used it for a similar purpose during the English Civil Wars but Parliamentary artillery badly damaged both the tower as well as the church's nave requiring them to be demolished. Rebuilding of these elements were undertaken between 1683-93 with the £9,000 (PDV £1.3 million) cost being raised by a nationwide appeal by King Charles II. The galleries were added and extended in 1708 and 1750 to accommodate the increased congregation. In 1927 the new diocese of Portsmouth was established out of Winchester resulting in design proposals to reflect the parish church of St Thomas of Canterbury's new status as a cathedral. The work was undertaken initially by Sir Charles Nicholson and later by Michael Drury with new aisles, tower, transepts and nave being commenced in 1935 but funding problems delayed its completion until 1991.

21. Ripon Cathedral (Cathedral status c686-709; 1836-present, built 671-8 and 1175-1522). The first clear evidence of a religious settlement in Ripon was a monastery dating from about 655AD. Its abbot Wilfrid employed continental masons in the design and construction of the abbey church, built between 671-8, with its crypt amazingly being preserved under the current cathedral. It is believed that Theodore created a fourth bishop in Northumbria at Ripon (to join York, Lindisfarne and Hexham) from about 686 which lasted until 709. The church was destroyed in 948 with its replacement suffering a similar fate. In 1154 Archbishop Roger of York gave £1,000 (circa £900,000) to rebuild it on a larger, continental style. The nave, parts of which are included in the current chapter house, and the surviving transepts date from 1175-81 probably by Arthur the Mason. The west front and accompanying towers were added in around 1230-40 with the east end reconfigured from 1288-97 paid by the granting of indulgencies to wealthy wrong-doers. The central tower was built in about 1460 following a collapse, the choir in c1482 whilst the rebuilt nave with added aisles, dating from 1502-22, are by Christopher Scune. In 1836 Ripon was given back its cathedral status after a break of some 1,150 years, the first change to the diocese map since the Reformation. The church has undergone restoration and alterations in 1829-34 by Edward Blore and by Sir George Gilbert Scott in 1861-9. In 2014, Ripon became a sub-division within the newly created diocese of West Yorkshire and the Dales, although it retains for the time being its cathedral status.

03. Rochester Cathedral (Cathedral status 604-616; c618-present, built 1077-1285, 1319-52, c1500-12). Rochester has been continually occupied since Neolithic times and became England's second oldest diocese (after Canterbury) when it was founded by one of Augustine's missionary's, Justus in 604. Excavation work in 1888-94 discovered the original cathedral which measures over 17 metres in length, consisted of a nave terminating with a circular apse at the east end. This church has been marked out on the ground around the present cathedral's western end. Corrupt rule immediately after the Norman Conquest almost bankrupted the small diocese until it was restored to financial health by Bishop Gundulf in 1077, who introduced Benedictine rule six years later initially with 22 monks. Building work commenced on the church immediately including the surviving crypt, north tower and nave which were completed in 1130. Three serious fires severely damaged the cathedral between 1133 and 1179 requiring restoration work. The west front dates c1150-60, presbytery, east transept and choir c1200-27 possibly by Richard the Mason, transepts and two east bays of the nave c1240-85. The central tower was added 1319-52 and Lady Chapel, unusually to the south side of the nave, in c1500-12 possibly by John Birch. Throughout its history lack of funds have meant rebuilding projects were either curtailed or cancelled, which has helped to preserve much of the cathedral's early fabric. After the monastery was dissolved in 1540 it was re-established as a secular cathedral in June 1541. Its dilapidated and neglected state was exacerbated by damage caused during the English Civil Wars. The cathedral underwent extensive Victorian restoration works including a rebuilt central tower in 1825 by Lewis Nockalls Cottingham, repair works supervised by Sir George Gilbert Scott from 1871 and J.L. Pearson in 1892. The tower was rebuilt again in 1904-5 under C. Hodgson Fowler.

44. Salisbury Cathedral (Cathedral status c1225-present, built 1220-66, tower and spire 1330-c80). Salisbury has been continuously occupied since Neolithic times. In 1219 it was decided to move the see from the unsuitable hill-fort of Old Sarum two miles away to the current one, then a greenfield site. Work commenced on a new cathedral in 1220 with the Lady Chapel finished in 1225, choir by 1237, transepts and nave by 1258 (by Nicholas of Ely and possibly also Elias of Dereham) and the west front in c1258-66 by Richard the Mason. It was therefore completed in only 46 years in one architectural style, Early English, a unique occurrence for an English medieval cathedral, at a cost of £28,000 (PDV £23.9 million). The non-monastic cloisters (c1263-84) and chapter house, begun in around 1275, were again by Richard the Mason. The cathedral's defining feature, its tower and spire, was added between 1330-c80 by Richard the Mason and Richard Farleigh from Wiltshire. At 123 metres in height it is the tallest surviving one in England and indeed the tallest structure in the country until the 1960's. The tower's masonry is 600mm thick at its base but only 225mm at its summit, weighed 6,000 tons and its supports had to be structurally enhanced between 1388 and 1423. The controversial church restorer James Wyatt removed two small chancery chapels and a detached 13th Century bell tower in 1787-93 as well as undertaking some 'tidying up' of the interior. A more sensitive restoration project was undertaken by Sir George Gilbert Scott from 1863. The cathedral houses the world's oldest working clock dating from 1386 as well as one of the four surviving copies of the Magna Carta.

77. Sheffield Cathedral (Cathedral status 1914-present, built c1430-1966). There has been a settlement in Sheffield since the Iron Age but it was its reputation for steel production that caused its rapid expansion of population in the 19th Century. The current cathedral site was first used for religious purposes in 1280 when Sheffield's second parish church was built here. This was demolished and rebuilt around 1430 on the standard cruciform shape to which the Shrewsbury chapel was added in about 1520 and a vestry chapel in 1777. The nave was rebuilt in 1804 and extended by some eight metres in 1880 along with both transepts, north and south by William Flockton. Further additions and alterations followed the parish churches rise in status to a cathedral in 1914 including the demolition and rebuilding of the nave and a new chancel on a north-south axis by Sir Charles Nicholson starting in 1936, which meant the current building is nearly three times the size of its predecessor. The Second World War delayed a scheme by architect Arthur Bailey to restore the churches original east-west axis which was not completed until 1966.

71. Southwell Minster (Cathedral status 1884-present, built 1108-50 and 1234-50). Southwell's first link to Christianity came when followers were baptised in the nearby river Trent with a church being built nearby in around 627. Land where the current minster stands was given by the Mercian king in 956 to the Archbishop of York with his former palace lying in ruins to the south of the cathedral. The resulting church was replaced following the Norman Conquest, which was started in 1108 with the surviving transepts, central tower and seven-bay nave completed by 1150. The extended six-bay eastern arm with ambulatory and eastern transepts were rebuilt from 1234-50 using the former Saxon church materials in its construction with its floor and parts of the north transept being included in their entirety. The chapter house was added between c1293-1300, the pulpitum c1320-35 and the insertion of windows to light the interior date from c1390-1450. The minster suffered little damage following the Reformation but did during the English Civil Wars when the nave was used to stable horses. In 1711 it suffered a lightning strike requiring spire, nave, tower and roofs to be repaired. It was used as a parish church in the mid-19th Century and underwent extensive restoration works by Ewan Christian from 1851. In 1884 the diocese of Nottinghamshire and Derbyshire was established and the minister became a cathedral, although the latter was transferred to Derby when a cathedral was founded there in 1927.

65. St Albans Cathedral (Cathedral status 1877-present, built 1077-1326, transepts facades and west front 1879-85). There is some evidence that the first church to be founded dates from as early as the 3rd Century in honour of England's first Christian martyr, St. Alban who was murdered in the second half of the century. Offa II, the King of Mercia, established a monastery in 793 on Holywell Hill near to the river Ver using materials from the adjacent and substantial Roman settlement of Verulamium. It was to become England's largest and most important in the early Middle Ages. Following Viking raids in 890 the monastery was vacated until St. Dunstan's Benedictine revival in the 970's. The current church dates from 1077 when building work commenced under a Norman known as Robertus the Mason. The design was influenced by what was being built in France at the time and used Roman and Saxon flint, limestone and Purbeck marble. It was completed in 1088 to become the largest church in England at the time. The central tower is the only one from this period still standing and survives along with most of the nave, transepts and the choir. The abbey was extended westwards including a more significant west front and lengthening the nave by three bays from 1195 until its completion in around 1235. At over 86 metres in length, the 13-bay nave is the longest of any existing medieval cathedral in England. Much of this work was undertaken by master mason Hugh de Godelif who was described as an untrustworthy and deceitful man but a consummate craftsman. The extended east end presbytery was started in 1235 including a new shrine to St Alban, retro-choir, ambulatory and a Lady Chapel, possibly by William Boyden. Lack of funds meant this work was not completed for a century after which five bays of the nave required rebuilding by Henry Wy following a collapse in 1323. Various works, like the great gatehouse, nave screen c1360-80 possibly by Henry Yeveley, the reredos and a chantry were constructed before the monastery was dissolved in 1539. The monastic buildings were plundered for their materials while the abbey church itself become a parish church. It was severely damaged during the English Civil Wars when it was used to house prisoners-of-war. Further storm damage meant that the abbey was in such a poor state that it was close to being demolished in the late 18th Century because it was deemed too large and costly to maintain. Extensive and much needed restoration work was undertaken by Sir George Gilbert Scott from 1856-77 being partly financed by a lawyer and amateur architect Lord Grimthorpe. After Scott's death Grimthorpe contributed £140,000 (£11.9 million) of his own money, restoring the nave as well as designing and adding controversial new terminations to the west end and to both transepts in 1879-85. In 1877 the diocese of St Albans was created with the abbey becoming a cathedral whilst also remaining as a parish church.

64. Truro Cathedral (Cathedral status 1876-present, built 1880-1910). When Truro cathedral was completed in 1910 it was the first one to be built on a new site in England since Salisbury with Cornwall regaining a separate diocese after a break of about 833 years. It was also the second new build Anglican cathedral to be built in England, 200 years after the first, St Paul's in London. Truro was selected as the bishop's seat in preference to the county town of Bodmin in 1876 with building work commencing four years later on the site of a 16th Century parish church which had to be largely demolished except for a section which was incorporated into the south-east corner of the current cathedral. It was designed in a Gothic Revival style by architect John Loughborough

Pearson who undertook several Victorian restoration commissions on other English cathedrals. The choir and transepts were complete by 1887 which allowed services to start replacing an adjacent temporary wooden structure which acted as a pro-cathedral for seven years. Following his death in 1897, his son F.L. Pearson supervised the building of the 76 metre tall central tower and spire (finished in 1905) and the two 61 metre high west towers in 1910. Only one bay of the proposed cloister was built in 1935 and a chapter house was added in 1967. The cathedral underwent restoration works in the 21st Century.

72. Wakefield Cathedral (Cathedral status 1888-present, mainly built between c1469-1905). The site of the current cathedral, built on a central hill in the city centre, has Anglo-Saxon origins with excavations in 1900 discovering the remains of a church from this period. The Normans built a replacement from around 1090, which was rebuilt in 1329 and again in 1469 when it was enlarged to include its 82 metre high tower and spire. Subsequently neglected following the Reformation, the church was restored and extended by George Gilbert Scott and his son between 1858-74. In 1888 the diocese of Wakefield was founded and the former All Saints parish church became a cathedral with the east end being subsequently extended in 1898-1905 by J.L. and his son F.L. Pearson. In 2014, Wakefield became a sub-division within the newly created diocese of West Yorkshire and the Dales although it retains for the time being its cathedral status.

25. Wells Cathedral (Cathedral status 909-1090 & 1245-present, built 1185-1435). Roman remains from the 4th or 5th centuries have been found on the present cathedral site in this small Somerset city, with the earliest church dating from 705 being located where the cloisters now stand. The diocese headquarters was moved to Wells from Sherborne in 909 before being transferred onto Bath in 1090. Despite this, work commenced on the current church in around 1185 starting with the choir followed by the transepts and nave with the north porch completed in c1230 all under the supervision of Adam Lock. Thomas Norreys added the west front from c1230-60 including the niches which were later to house the 350 or so statues, half of which are life-sized or larger and were originally coloured and richly decorated. These date from the late 13th Century and include saints, apostles, kings, bishops as well as biblical and legendary figures. Wells regained its cathedral status in 1245, when it was believed the cathedral was also consecrated. Wells held the bishopric jointly with Bath until 1539 and solely from then on even though the diocese continues to be known as Bath and Wells. The 52 metre diameter octagonal chapter house was added c1310-9 and the central tower c1315-22, both probably by Thomas Witney. The choir, retro-choir and five-sided Lady Chapel were reconstructed in c1329-45 by local mason William Joy with the money raised by local taxes. So unpopular were these that the church was forced to build a perimeter wall with moat and drawbridge to give it added protection. The controversial scissor-like strainer arches to reinforce and support the distressed central crossing tower are also attributed to Joy and were built c1338-55. The south-west tower was added by William Wynford in 1367-86 and the north-west tower dates from c1425-35. The cloisters were built in various stages from c1420-1508, two phases by William Smyth and William Atwood. Following the Reformation, the eastern chantries were abolished and fittings and fixtures removed. The cathedral suffered only minor damage during the English Civil Wars. A major restoration programme was undertaken during the Victorian era and this continued into the 20th Century with works to the west end. Wells also has a large number of outstanding secular outbuildings that survived the Reformation including the renowned Vicars' Close.

13. Winchester Cathedral (Cathedral status c660-present, built 1079-1532). Winchester developed into one of the five most important towns in Roman England becoming the capital of the Anglo-Saxon kingdom of Wessex and effectively of England for a time. The original church known as Old Minster dates from 642 and was located just to the north of the current cathedral's nave when Winchester replaced Dorchester-on-Thames as the seat of the bishop of Wessex in around 660. Two further churches, known as New and Nuns Minsters, were built to the north of the Old Minster in 890 and 903 respectively. A Benedictine monastery was added in around 965 and the Old Minster was demolished in 1093 when the current cathedral was consecrated. This church was started in 1079 with the limestone transported from Bumstead on the Isle of Wight with the surviving crypt and transepts being completed in 1093 possibly by Hugh the Mason. The body of King William II was interned here in 1100 joining six earlier Anglo-Saxon kings. The tower and adjoining north and south bays were replaced in c1120 following a 1107 collapse, while the retro-choir and Lady Chapel were built 1202-c35 probably by masons Richard and Stephen. The presbytery dating from c1315-60 was rebuilt by Thomas Witney, the nave was reduced by 13 metres and a new west front built along with north and south aisles from c1367. The nave was re-faced in a Perpendicular style and Wykeham's chapel was constructed from 1394-c1450 by William Wynford and Robert Hulle. Further works included an eastern extension to the Lady Chapel (c1490-1500), the remodelling around the presbytery and an additional chantry chapel (c1520-32) by Thomas Berry. Following the dissolution of the monastery in 1538, it became a secular cathedral in March, 1541. The cloisters and chapter house were subsequently demolished and the cathedral's fixtures and fittings destroyed. The church underwent restoration works in three phases between 1812 and 1912, the last by Sir Thomas Graham Jackson. At 181.75 metres, Winchester is the longest English medieval cathedral still standing.

17. Worcester Cathedral (Cathedral status c679-present, mainly built 1084-1504). Worcester was developed by the Romans although the settlement pre-dates this being an important crossing point over the river Severn. In around 679 the abbey church of St Peter, which probably stood just north of the present College Green, become a cathedral when the diocese was founded. It was reformed as a Benedictine monastery in the late 960's with another church in the same location, St Mary, becoming the cathedral after being rebuilt in about 983. Building work on the current cathedral started in 1084 directed by Wulstan who was the only Anglo-Saxon bishop to retain his position following the Norman Conquest even though he objected to the demolition of its predecessor. The crypt, completed in 1092, survives from this period as does the distinctive circular chapter house built from c1120. The church acted as a refuge for local people during a civil war in 1113 which disrupted building work. Seven bays of the nave were complete by c1170 with two further ones added between 1170-5. The cathedral suffered a series of catastrophes including an 1176 central tower collapse, a 1202 fire and a 1222 storm. The body of the much maligned King John was interned here in 1216. The east end was rebuilt, double in size including a Lady Chapel, from 1224-c69 by Alexander the Mason and this work continued into the rest of the nave including the central tower (1317-75) by William of Shockerwick and John Clyve. The later was responsible for the west front and commencing the cloisters between 1372-95. The cloisters were completed in two further phases, first from 1404-32 and then 1435-8 by John Chapman. A chantry chapel for Prince Arthur, eldest son of Henry VII who died just five months after marrying Princess Katherine of Aragon in 1501, completed the cathedral's build in 1502-4. Following the dissolution of the monastery in 1540 it became a secular cathedral in January 1542 with major restoration work being carried out by A.E. Perkins (1857-69) and Sir George Gilbert Scott in 1870-4.

05. York Minster (Cathedral status c627-33; 664-present, built c1230-1472). York is second only to Canterbury in terms of religious importance, being the headquarters of the Archbishop of York who is responsible for the Anglican church in northern England. The city was founded in 71AD as Eboracum by the Romans and has a long Christian history sending a bishop to a Council in Arles as early as 314AD. It became the capital of Northumbria in the Anglo-Saxon period and later grew in wealth and population thanks to wool, the railways and confectionary. The current cathedral was built on the site of the Roman fort, the remains of which have been discovered, and which probably contained a building for Christian worship. The first recorded church dates from 627 when Augustine missionaries built a modest timber cathedral and baptised the King of Northumbria. This was soon replaced by a stone basilica before the see was abandoned for Lindisfarne in 633, not being re-established again until about 664. The church was destroyed by fire in 741 and rebuilt on a grander scale. It appears then to have fallen into disrepair before being repaired when it became a monastery as part of Dunstan's 10th Century Benedictine revival. The cathedral suffered damage in the northern uprisings opposing Norman rule between 1069-75 and its 1080 replacement was destroyed by fire in 1137. A major rebuild started in 1154-81 with just four piers in the crypt visible today. The potential wealth of the archbishopric enabled the cathedral to be designed in the new Gothic style, to a comparable scale to Canterbury and those found in Europe. This work commenced in around 1230 but financial problems delayed its completion for nearly 250 years. The north and south transepts (c1230-41) were built first before the chapter house, England's largest, was added between c1265-96. The nave and west front were built 1291-1345 by Simon the Mason while the west window from c1330-8 is by Ivo de Raghton. The new east arm, which exceeded the nave in length, commenced in 1361 and took over 60 years to complete. This included the four-bays of retro-choir, ambulatory and the Lady Chapel (1361-72) by William Hoton and Robert Patrington and the five-bay sanctuary and choir (c1380-1410) by Hugh Hedon. The 25 metre high by 11 metres wide great east window was glazed by John Thornton of Coventry between 1405-8 is full of Christian symbolism and is exceeded only in size by the one found in Gloucester Cathedral. The central tower, which collapsed in 1407, was initially rebuilt between 1408-23 by William Colchester. The south-west tower (1432-56) is by Thomas Pak whilst the north-west tower and heightened central tower (1470-2) are by William Hyndeley. Like all religious buildings, the Reformation resulted in the removal and destruction of all Roman Catholic fixtures and fittings with the cathedral suffering further damage during the English Civil Wars. An arson attack on the choir in 1829 resulted in £65,000 (PDV £6.8 million) of damage whilst another fire in the south-west tower in 1840 required £23,000 (£2.4 million) to repair. These disasters, along with financial problems, meant the state of the cathedral got so bad that in the 1850's religious services had to be suspended. Much needed restoration works were undertaken by G.E. Street from 1875-80, G.F. Bodley (1887-1911) and major structural enhancements by Bernard Feilden in 1966-72. York is the largest in terms of area of any English medieval cathedral as well as being its widest by 15 metres.

England's 28 Former Cathedrals

39. Bath Abbey (Cathedral status c1090-1539, built c1496-1610). Bath predates the Roman occupation when it became an important spa town from the 1st Century AD. An early nunnery dating from 676 and a late 8th Century house for secular canons was destroyed by Danish invaders before being reformed under Dunstan's Benedictine revival in around 970. The abbey was rebuilt by the Normans from c1090, when it became a cathedral for the diocese of Somerset, being largely completed in 1170. Bath shared the see with Glastonbury from 1195 until 1218 and with Wells from 1245 to 1539. Bishops, however, preferred the alternative venues which resulted in Bath becoming severely neglected and run-down. The abbey was eventually completely demolished and rebuilt between c1496-1539 on the site of the former church's nave by royal masons Robert and William Vertue following a high profile campaign to raise funds. In an unfortunate piece of timing, the unfinished cathedral and its adjoining priory was dissolved in January 1539 and its lands sold off. In 1572 the incomplete abbey became the parish church of St Peter and St Paul after being purchased by a wealthy benefactor, Edmund Colthurst who completed it in around 1610. Extensive restoration works were undertaken between 1833-1901 by George Philip Manners, Sir George Gilbert Scott and Sir Thomas Graham Jackson. The latter added the cloister-like structure between 1924-6. A 'Heritage Vaults' museum in the old cellars contains some masonry fragments from the Norman cathedral. Even though the see was transferred to Wells in 1539, the diocese continues to be known as Bath and Wells with the current church remaining as Bath Abbey.

23. Bodmin Parish Church (Cathedral status c865?-c900? and c930?-c960?). The earliest reliable evidence of a monastery at Bodmin dates from around 865 when it appears Bishop Kenstec declared his allegiance to the Archbishop of Canterbury resulting in Cornwall becoming an English diocese. It is probable that Bodmin or Launceston housed the bishop's seat until around 900. When the Cornish see was re-established again in around 930 it was either located at Bodmin or more likely at St Germans which was certainly the case from about 960. It is believed the current parish church of St. Petroc, which was built 1469-72, occupies the site of the earlier monastic cathedral.

11. Bradwell-on-Sea (St. Peter-on-the-Wall - Cathedral status c654-c675). When the Bishop of London was expelled from his city base in around 616, he was forced to set up his diocese headquarters in a safer place eventually choosing the former Roman fort of Orthona near Bradwell-on-Sea, Essex in which to build a modest pro-cathedral in c654. Subsequently abandoned, the church was later used as a barn before being restored and re-consecrated as the chapel of St. Peter-on-the-Wall in 1920. The chapel is still used today, being rectangular in shape with its apse and side chapels having been removed and a three-arch opening at the east-end bricked up.

01. Canterbury (St Martin's church - Cathedral status c597-c602). The church of St Martin was used as Augustine's mission church from c597 until Canterbury Cathedral's completion in around 602. The current church's nave dates from this period with other parts pre-dating this although the apse and tower were added much later. St Martin's is still used as a parish church making this England's longest continually-used Christian building as well as its oldest former cathedral.

36. Chester St. John Baptist Church (Cathedral status 1075-c1102). The original church on the site dates from around 689. It is thought the Normans started to build a substantial replacement just prior to it becoming a cathedral when the Mercian bishopric was moved here from Lichfield in 1075. Its cathedral status lasted only between 20 and 27 years before the bishop's seat was moved to Coventry and the church returned to its former use served by secular canons. The church itself was not completed until the 12th Century with the central crossing, the reduced chancel, transepts and nave still visible in today's parish church. The establishment was closed in 1547 when a tower collapsed causing extensive damage to the nave. It suffered further damage during the English Civil Wars with parts of the demolished east and west ends visible as ruins today. The church was restored in the 17th Century but the tower collapsed again in 1881 requiring another rebuild on a more modest scale. Further restoration works were undertaken between 1859-66 by R.C. Hussey. The church possesses a collection of interesting pre-Conquest artefacts which are on display. Even though the exterior is unremarkable and much changed, the interior gives a rare glimpse into what a smaller-scale Norman cathedral would have looked like.

24. Chester-le-Street (Durham) (Cathedral status c883-995). The ex-Roman fort town became the home of monks, treasures and the body of their revered Bishop Cuthbert, when Lindisfarne was destroyed and abandoned following Viking raids in about 883. The monks erected a timber church and it became the seat of the bishop until it was moved onto Durham in 995. The site of the cathedral is unclear but it could be where the current collegiate church of St Mary and St Cuthbert stands which dates from the 12th Century. The splendid 53 metre high spire was added in the 1400's.

40. Coventry St Mary's Priory (Cathedral status c1102-[c1143-1248?]-1539). Coventry's St Mary's Priory was a small Benedictine monastery founded in the 1020's with its abbey completed in around 1043. It was rebuilt and enlarged by the Normans after the bishop's seat was moved here from Chester sometime between 1087 and 1102. Civil war and a dispute with Lichfield over the election of the bishop meant that neither controlled the diocese between about 1143 and 1248. This dispute was settled with both agreeing to hold the see jointly. The settlement was closed in January 1539 and it became, along with Osney, only England's second cathedral to be completely destroyed as part of the Reformation. Its materials were sold off and what remains of the settlement is today open to the public.

26. Crediton (Devon) (Cathedral status 909-c1050). The Devon village of Crediton dates from Anglo-Saxon times and a monastery was established here in around 739. It became the diocese headquarters for Devon in 909 when it was formed out of the see of Sherborne. It subsumed the diocese of Cornwall in about 1043 before being transferred onto Exeter in 1050. Crediton continued as a collegiate church being rebuilt in the 12th Century. The collegiate arrangement was dissolved in about 1547 and the church sold to local villagers who have used the extended and altered building as a parish church ever since. It is probable that the Anglo-Saxon cathedral was largely built of timber and lies beneath the present church although a recent archaeological investigation has proved inconclusive.

08. Dommoc (Cathedral status c630-c870). Considerable doubt surrounds the location of the cathedral for East Anglia which existed from around 630 until about 870 when it was abandoned following Danish raids. We do know it was based at Dommoc but we do not know where Dommoc was located. It could have been at either Old Felixstowe or Dunwich but no remains of a cathedral have been discovered and, in Dunwich's case, the town itself has disappeared beneath the sea due to coastal erosion. The East Anglican diocese was divided in 673 when a second one was created at Elmham.

10. Dorchester-on-Thames (Cathedral status 635-660; c680-c779 & c870-1072). The original cathedral for the Anglo-Saxon kingdom of Wessex, was established in this small, isolated riverside Oxfordshire town in 635 until the bishopric was moved to Winchester in 660. Some 20 years later it was re-established for south Mercia (not Wessex as previous) which lasted until c779. After the Danish invaders made the sees at Leicester and Lindsey uninhabitable, the cathedral for the whole of Mercia was based here from around 870 with its massive diocese now stretching from the river Thames to the river Humber in the north. This remained the case until 1072 when the Normans removed it to Lincoln. After losing its bishop, the settlement became an Augustinian abbey in 1140 and became a place of pilgrimage after a shrine was erected in honour of its first Bishop, Birinus in 1225. This resulted in the church being rebuilt and extended but it remained a financially poor monastery until its demise in 1536. Apart from a later tower and the removal of part of a transept, the current large parish church remains intact, incorporating masonry fragments from as far back as the Anglo-Saxon era. The only remaining monastic building is currently used as a museum.

15. Elmham (Cathedral status c673-c870). The East Anglican see at Elmham was created out of Dommoc in around 673 until Viking raids meant it also had to be abandoned in the late 9th Century. Considerable doubt surrounds its location with some historians suggesting that it could be at North Elmham whilst others favour South Elmham, 30 miles to the south in Suffolk. The later has a potential site known locally as Old Minister which has the remains of a flint wall but possesses no identifiable architectural features.

43. Glastonbury Abbey (Cathedral status 1195-1218). Glastonbury is situated on a raised area above the flood plains of Somerset and has been continuously inhabited since Neolithic times. Its earliest religious significance is disputed but Roman remains have been found around the abbey and the site is inextricably linked to the legends of King Arthur, Queen Guinevere and the Holy Grail. The area was occupied by Saxons from Wessex in 658 who enriched the settlement and built a new church from around 712, parts of which can still be seen in the standing remains. The monastery was enlarged as part of St Dunstan's 10th Century monastery revival but it was the Normans who greatly enhanced and rebuilt both the church and the monastery following their Conquest of 1066. A fire in 1186 resulted in further restoration works just before the abbey church become a cathedral in 1195 which it shared with Bath until 1218. Glastonbury became one of England's two wealthiest monasteries until it was controversially closed as part of the Dissolution of the Monasteries in 1539. In a rare show of defiance, the last abbot Richard Whyting and two of his monks were executed for treason on St Michael's Tor after refusing to surrender. Today Glastonbury is one of England's most revered sacred sites with significant remains of the 65 metre long church, Lady Chapel and the restored Abbot's kitchen, all of which are open to the public along with a museum containing some interesting artefacts. The bodies of three Anglo-Saxon kings are also buried here.

19. Hexham Parish Church (Cathedral status c680-c875). The town's strategic location has meant it was extremely susceptible to conflicts suffering Viking,

Scottish and Wars of the Roses damage. A monastery with an abbey was established in Hexham by Wilfrid, the Bishop of York, in 674 before his expulsion from Northumbria three years later. In c680 the diocese of Northumbria was split by Theodore with Hexham joining York and Lindisfarne in possessing cathedrals. Viking raids, however, meant that Hexham's cathedral status lasted only until c875. Astonishingly, like Ripon, the crypt survives from this period along with Roman and Anglo-Saxon fixtures including a stone seat, carved cross and chalice plus some rare 15th Century wall paintings. An Augustinian priory was founded in about 1131 with the choir, both transepts and the cloisters all built from 1180-1250 now forming part of the current church. The old nave, however, was destroyed following the Reformation and the priory was dissolved in 1537 when it became a parish church. The east end and nave were rebuilt by Temple Moore and the choir restored from 1860 until 1908. Remains of the cloister and a gatehouse are visible today.

29. Hoxne (Suffolk) (Cathedral status c950-c1070). The Bishop of London created an East Anglian see at Hoxne in around 950, which it shared with North Elmham from 1040. This arrangement lasted until it was re-united at North Elmham just prior to it moving to Thetford in 1072. The former cathedral was known as the church of St. Peter and is believed to be on the same site as the present parish church of St. Peter and St. Paul although no remains have been discovered. Hoxne Priory, located just under a mile to the south of this church, is an alternative, if less likely venue.

18. Leicester (Cathedral status c679 but certainly by 737-c870). Leicester hosted a bishop in Mercia during the Anglo-Saxon era probably from around 679 but definitely by 737, until approximately 870 when it was moved to the more secure and isolated Dorchester-on-Thames following Viking raids. It is unknown where this cathedral stood but the most likely site is where the current St. Nicholas parish church stands which incorporates some Roman materials and dates from around 900. The tower is early Norman while the building underwent extensive restoration works between 1875-84.

09. Lindisfarne (Cathedral status 635-664; c678-c875). Commonly known as Holy Island, Lindisfarne was founded as a base in England for the Celtic strand of Christianity from Ireland and Scotland in 635, becoming a cathedral after the abandonment of York. It is believed the church at this time was built of timber and had a thatched roof. The see returned to York in 664 before two more bishoprics were created for Northumbria first here in c678 and at Hexham some two years later. Cuthbert, Lindisfarne's bishop for only three years, was enshrined as early as 698. The monastery was famous for literacy with the

'Lindisfarne Gospels' (now in the British Museum) being written here. Holy Island suffered from repeated Viking raids in the early 9th Century before finally being abandoned in about 875. The monks took St Cuthbert's body, their treasures and the bishop's seat to Durham in 995 after a stay lasting over one hundred years in Chester-le-Street. Lindisfarne was re-established as a Benedictine priory by the Normans in 1093 which continued until its enforced closure in 1536. Today the ruins of this later monastery are open to the public along with the current parish church of St. Mary's which stands on the original settlement.

06. Lindsey, Lincolnshire (Cathedral status c628-33; c677-c870; c950; c958). We do know a diocese was first set up in Lindsey by Paulinus in around 628 which lasted for only a few years. Excavations in Lincoln's Roman forum on the site of the current church of St Paul-in-the-Bail to the west of the cathedral in the late 1970's revealed foundations similar to the 7th Century church found next to Rochester cathedral. It is believed these are the remains of the Paulinus church. The Lindsey see was re-established following Theodore's 7th Century revival but as no remains have been found of this later cathedral in Lincoln, this has led to speculation that it was located elsewhere with Caistor, Louth, Horncastle and Stow all being suggested. The Vikings destroyed the settlement in around 870 when the Mercian see was moved to the more secure Dorchester-on-Thames. It is believed the Lindsey bishopric was twice briefly re-established again in the middle of the 10th Century.

45. London - Westminster Abbey (Cathedral status 1540-50, built 1245-1512 and 1698-1745). Westminster Abbey is arguably the most important surviving medieval church in England playing host to numerous royal, state and civic occasions going back to before the Norman Conquest of 1066. The abbey became a cathedral when it became the seat of the Bishop of Middlesex for ten years from 1540 following the closure of its monastery. Except for this brief period the abbey has been known as a 'Royal Peculiar' being under the jurisdiction of the monarch and is therefore not part of the Church of England's diocese constitution. All monarchs have been crowned here since 1066, 17 were buried here from 1066 until 1760, as have distinguished politicians, scientists, poets and writers: Chaucer, Dickens, Newton, Darwin, Wilberforce, Pitt as well as an unidentified soldier killed in the First World War who was interned in the 'Tomb of the Unknown Soldier' in 1920. The first church built on the site, then known as Thorney island, dates from the 7th Century before St Dunstan founded a Benedictine monastery called St. Peter's Abbey in around 958. King Edward the Confessor paid for the church to be rebuilt in a Romanesque style and to a scale similar to those found in Normandy where he had been raised and educated. It was commenced in 1050, consecrated in 1065 but not fully complete until 1090. Only fragments of this church and its Anglo-Saxon predecessor survive. Work began on the current abbey on 6th July, 1245 with the octagonal chapter house and east end. By 1259 the presbytery housing the shrine of Edward the Confessor, the ambulatory, transepts and chapter house were complete with five bays of the nave by 1272. These works cost a staggering £40,000 (PDV £34.2 million). Work on completing the nave recommenced in 1376 by royal mason Henry Yeveley and continued up until 1471 although its roof and west front were not finished until 1502. The Lady Chapel was replaced between 1503-12 with the Henry VII chapel, costing £20,000 (£11 million) by royal master mason Robert Janyns. Up until its dissolution, the monastery was England's wealthiest helped by royal patronage and its proximity to the seat of government at nearby Westminster Palace. Under Queen Mary's Catholic reign, the monastery was briefly restored in 1556 served by an abbot and 14 monks before finally being closed down for good in 1560 under Elizabeth I's sovereignty. Like most religious buildings, it suffered damage during and immediately after the English Civil Wars but exceptionally most monastic buildings survived. The two west towers were added by architect Nicholas Hawksmoor between 1698-1745 with some subsequent restoration and rebuilding works being undertaken by Sir George Gilbert Scott.

30. North Elmham (Cathedral status c955-1072). Elmham housed the bishop's seat for the East Angles from approximately 673 until the middle of the 9th Century before Viking raids made the site uninhabitable. There is considerable doubts whether this was based here in a rural village near to the river Wensum or in nearby South Elmham. It is believed, however, a cathedral was created at North Elmham in the middle of the 10th Century, sharing the East Anglian see with Hoxne from about 1040 for 30 years before it was briefly re-united again here and eventually moved to Thetford in 1072. Excavations have revealed a timber structure which are possibly those of the Saxon cathedral dating from this period. This was later replaced by a private chapel for Bishop Herbert de Losinga sometime between 1091 and 1119. In the 14th Century, Bishop Henry le Despencer turned the chapel into a manor house which he later fortified following the Peasants' Revolt in 1381. The remains of the chapel and house are today visible above ground with the site being open to the public courtesy of English Heritage.

37. Old Sarum, Salisbury (Cathedral status 1075-c1225). Old Sarum, some two miles north of Salisbury, was an Iron Age hill fort later occupied by the Romans and Anglo-Saxons. The Normans moved the see here from Sherborne in 1075 because of its fortifications with the cathedral being completed in 1092.

It was far smaller than most other contemporary Norman cathedrals consisting of a standard cruciform shape with nave, apse, central tower and several chapels but just five days after it was consecrated a storm caused extensive damage. It is believed that lack of an adequate water supply, its exposed location and problems between the clergy and the military who occupied the neighbouring castle meant that the bishop's seat was moved to the new partly built Salisbury Cathedral in around 1225. Old Sarum was subsequently demolished and the materials were used to build the new cathedral close. The Lady Chapel was used for a century or so before the whole settlement was abandoned at the end of the 16th Century. The site is open to the public where the outline of the old cathedral is visible on the ground as are the remains of the adjoining castle.

50. Osney (Oxfordshire) (Cathedral status 1542-6). Osney (formerly Oseney) Island is located next to the river Thames to the west of Oxford. An Augustinian priory stood here from 1129, with the abbey dating from 1154 until it was closed in 1539. In the 13th Century it became one of the most important Augustinian houses in the country, served by as many as 50 canons. The abbey church, predominately dating from the 13th Century with a tall west tower, became a cathedral in 1542 for the diocese of Oxfordshire which was created out of Lincoln's massive see. This status lasted for just four years before being moved to Christ Church, Oxford in 1546. Gradually stripped of its materials, its masonry was used to reinforce Oxford's defences during the English Civil Wars. It rapidly became a ruin so that now only one small 15th Century building remains with the rest of the site being used as a graveyard. Osney is, along with Coventry, the only English cathedral to have been completely destroyed as a result of the Reformation.

27. Ramsbury (Cathedral status 909-1058), Ramsbury was created for the see of Wiltshire in about 909 out of the Winchester bishopric and this remained the case until it was eventually moved to Old Sarum via Sherborne in 1058. The Saxon cathedral is believed to have been built of timber and located on the site of the present parish church of the Holy Cross. The settlement continued as a Benedictine monastery after its status change until it was finally dissolved and sold off as a parish church in 1539. The main structure of the current church dates from the 15th Century and the surviving parts of the monastery are now used as a school.

12. Repton (Derbyshire) (Possible cathedral status c655-c669). The original see for the Saxon kingdom of Mercia was probably based in its most important town, Repton with the Celtic monastery housing both monks and nuns from around 655 until it was moved to Lichfield in 669. Viking raids destroyed the settlement but it was reformed as an Augustinian priory from 1153 until 1538. The neighbouring St. Wynstan's church is of a later date than the 7th Century cathedral but it does contain a Saxon crypt and some royal Mercian relics.

20. Selsey (Cathedral status c681-1075). The exiled Bishop of York, Wilfrid, established a monastery here in Church Norton in around 680, with Selsey becoming the headquarters for the South Saxon see a year or so later until it was moved onto Chichester in 1075. The site of the Saxon cathedral is uncertain with some sources claiming it has been submerged under the sea whilst others say it was located where the original monastery stood. This site housed a church that was rebuilt in the 13th Century and its chancel, known as St. Wilfrid's chapel, was physically moved two miles to its current location in the centre of Church Norton in 1865.

22. Sherborne Abbey (Cathedral status 705-1075). Sherborne Abbey's history dates from 705 when the King of Wessex founded a second see here to serve the west of his kingdom which lasted until it was moved to Old Sarum in 1075. Its diocese was reduced in size to cover only Dorset in 909 when bishoprics were created at Crediton, Ramsbury and Wells. Sherborne became a Benedictine monastery from 998 until it was dissolved in 1539 after which the abbey become a parish church and the monastery buildings a school. A former parish church, located next to the abbey, was demolished and its foundations are visible today. There are fragments in the current abbey of early 11th Century Anglo-Saxon and Norman remains while two Anglo-Saxon kings are buried here. The Lady Chapel was added in the 13th Century and the choir rebuilt in 1490.

07. Soham (Cambridgeshire) (Possible cathedral c630 & again c900). There is speculation that a monastery was founded in the Cambridgeshire village of Soham in around 630 and became a cathedral very briefly for the East Anglia diocese just prior to the establishment of Dommoc. When Dommoc and Elmham were abandoned because of Viking raids, some sources maintain that the see was re-established here again in around 900. Traces of Saxon masonry are visible in the town's parish church of St. Andrew's but it cannot be assumed this proves the existence of any earlier cathedral on the site.

28. St Germans Priory (Cathedral status c930? or c960-c1032 and 1046-50). It is believed Cornwall's first see in the middle of the 9th Century was based at either Bodmin or Launceston. In around 930 but certainly from the middle of the 10th Century, the Cornish bishopric was re-established at St Germans before being united with Devon and moved to Crediton in around 1032. Its diocese appears to have been re-formed briefly in the middle of the 11th Century before finally being settled in Exeter. The present parish church occupies the site of the Anglo-Saxon cathedral which was demolished and replaced by a grander church when it became an Augustinian priory in 1184. Parts of the twin-towered west front date from this period whilst the priory was closed and sold off in 1539.

34. Thetford (Cathedral status 1072-1094). The bishopric of East Anglia was transferred to the more important town of Thetford from the isolated village of North Elmham in 1072 before it finally moved onto Norwich in 1094. Nothing remains of the cathedral as it was probably built of timber and even its location is uncertain. The best guess is that it was built on the site of an earlier settlement known as St Mary the Greater which was vacated and later became a Dominican friary in 1335 before being finally closed in 1538. Thetford Grammar school have occupied this site since 1566 and recent excavations have revealed some 11th and 12th Century masonry.

England's 33 Cathedrals of non-Anglican Denominations

94. Aldershot (Cathedral status 1972-present; built 1892/93). The church was originally built in 1892/3 by Sir Robert Lorimer as an Anglican church for the local British Army garrison, converting to a Roman Catholic one in 1972 before becoming a cathedral for the 'Roman Catholic Bishop of the Forces.'

91. Arundel (Diocese established 1965-present; built 1870-3). The 15th Duke of Norfolk commissioned Joseph A. Hansom to design a Roman Catholic parish church for his Arundel estate which was built between 1870-3. It became a cathedral in 1965 for the newly created Roman Catholic diocese of Arundel and Brighton.

53. Birmingham (Diocese established 1850-present; built 1839-41). The parish church was built between 1839-41 with the tower added in 1856 to a design by Augustus W.N. Pugin, becoming a Roman Catholic cathedral for the newly formed diocese of Birmingham in 1850. It underwent a controversial restoration in 1967 which resulted in the destruction of many of Pugin's fixtures and finishes.

89. Birmingham (Cathedral status 1958-present; built 1873). A Greek Orthodox cathedral was established in 1958 having formerly been a Catholic Apostolic church designed in 1873 by architect J.A. Chatwin. It has undergone some 21st Century restoration works.

78. Brentwood (Diocese established 1917-present; built 1858-61 & 1989-91). Originally built as a Roman Catholic church between 1858-61 to a design by

Gilbert Blount, it became a Catholic cathedral in 1917. It was extended and radically altered between 1972-4 by John Newton who changed the church's axis. Unfortunately this new work had unsurmountable structural problems and had to be demolished. The cathedral was rebuilt, courtesy of a large anonymous donation, by architect Quinlan Terry in 1989-91 with most of the original church being incorporated into the design.

54. Clifton (Bristol) (Diocese established 1850-present; built 1970-3). A much troubled parish church was built between 1834-48 by H.E. Goodridge which became a Roman Catholic cathedral when the diocese of Bristol was established in the suburb of Clifton in 1850. It was, however, never fully finished or indeed even consecrated and has since been converted into offices and flats. The current Roman Catholic cathedral stands on a different site and was built between 1970-3 by architectural practice Percy Thomas Partnership.

82. Lancaster (Diocese established 1924-present; built 1857-9). A chapel was built on the current site in 1767, being replaced by a Roman Catholic parish church in 1857-9 to a design by E.G. Paley at a reported cost of £15,000 (£1.35 million). It became a Roman Catholic cathedral in 1924 when the diocese was established and underwent a major refurbishment in the mid-1990's.

66. Leeds (Diocese established 1878-present; built 1902-4). The Dominicans founded a chapel in 1793 which was replaced in 1838 by St Anne's Roman Catholic church designed by John Child before becoming a Catholic cathedral in 1878. A road widening scheme meant the church had to be demolished and a new one was built on a different site between 1902-4 to designs by John Henry Eastwood and S.K. Greenslade. The present Lady Chapel contains fixtures and fittings by A.W.N. Pugin from the earlier cathedral.

55. Liverpool (Diocese established 1850-present; built 1962-7). The Roman Catholic diocese was founded in 1850 to cater for the Irish immigrants coming to Liverpool to escape the Great Potato Famine (1845-52) and attempts to build a cathedral resulted in two aborted schemes spanning over a century. While this was happening, St Nicholas church (built 1813-5, demolished in 1973) was used as a temporary or pro-cathedral. Lack of money curtailed the first proposal to build a massive cathedral in Everton, designed by Edward Pugin, in which only the Lady Chapel was completed before its abandonment in 1856. This chapel was later demolished in the 1980's. An even larger scheme was proposed by Sir Edwin Lutyens and was commenced in 1933. This church was to be the second biggest in the World, being even longer (at 227 metres) with a dome even larger than St Peter's Basilica in Rome. The Second World War and financial reality (its cost rose nine-fold to £27 million PDV £1,194 million in

1941) meant only the crypt was completed by 1958. In 1960 Frederick Gibberd won an architectural competition to design cathedral mark three which was built in only five years between 1962-7 over Lutyens crypt. Its innovative design created structural and water leakage problems requiring extensive and expensive restoration works which were undertaken between 1992 and 2003.

96. London (Camberwell) (Cathedral status 1977-present; built 1873). A Greek Orthodox cathedral since 1977, purchased in 1963, it was originally a Catholic Apostolic church dating from 1873 designed by J and J. Belcher.

101. London (Camden Town) (Cathedral status 1991-present; built 1822-4). A former Church of England parish church built 1822-4 to designs by father and son William and Henry Inwood, it was not dedicated until 1920. It was sold in 1948 becoming a Greek Orthodox cathedral in 1991.

102. London (Chiswick) (Cathedral status 1999; built 1997-9). After leasing for several years, the Russian Orthodox Church Outside Russia commissioned the design and building of a new cathedral which was erected between 1997-9, being consecrated in 2007.

97. London (Golders Green) (Cathedral status 1979-present; built 1914-25 & 1960). A Greek Orthodox cathedral since 1979 which it shared with the Anglicans from 1970. It was originally built in 1914/15 to designs by J.T. Lee with extensions added in 1924/5 and 1960.

88. London Cathedral (Kensington) (Cathedral status 1956-present; built 1848-92). This church became a Russian Orthodox cathedral for the Diocese of Sourozh in 1956 after being originally built as the Anglican church of All Saints in 1848/9 to a design by Lewis Vulliamy. Its bell tower was added in 1860 while its west façade was remodelled in 1891/2.

93. London (Kentish Town) (Cathedral status 1970-present; built 1884/85 & 1961-70). A Greek Orthodox cathedral was founded in 1970 following a nine-year adaptation. It was originally the Anglican church of St Barnabas built in 1884/5 by Ewan Christian.

92. London (Mayfair) (Cathedral status 1968-present; built 1889-91). The Ukrainian Catholic Cathedral of Holy Family in Exile was purchased from the United Congregational church in 1967, becoming a cathedral a year later. The church was designed by architect Alfred Waterhouse and was built in 1889-91.

100. London Cathedral (Regent's Park) (Cathedral status 1989-present; built 1836/7). Built in 1836/7 for the Anglican church by James Pennethorne, it became the Antiochian Orthodox cathedral of St George in 1989.

90. London (Shepherd's Bush) (Cathedral status 1963-present; built 1882-87). A Greek Orthodox cathedral since the 1963, it was formerly the Anglican church of St Thomas, built between 1882-87 to a design by A.W. Blomfield.

62. London (Southwark) (Diocese established 1850-present; built 1838-48). The Roman Catholic church of St. George was designed by Augustus W.N. Pugin and built between 1838-48 just prior to it becoming a cathedral in 1850. It was badly damaged during the Second World War before being restored by Romilly B. Craze between 1953-8 with the adjoining Amigo Hall being used as a temporary or pro-cathedral during this period.

63. London (Westminster) (Diocese established 1850-present; built 1895-1903). The country's largest and most important Catholic church is the headquarters of the Roman Catholic faith in England and Wales as well as being the seat of the Archbishop of Westminster. The diocese was founded in 1850, one of the 11 original ones following Catholic emancipation. The current cathedral was built 1895-1903, although it was not consecrated until 1910, in a Byzantine style to contrast with the nearby Anglican Westminster Abbey. It was designed by architect John F. Bentley and the church is faced with striking orange brick and white stone bandings with its campanile being 95 metre tall.

81. London (Westminster) (Cathedral status 1922-present; built 1877-82). The only purpose built Greek Orthodox cathedral in England, the Church of St Sophia in Moscow Road, Bayswater is the denominations mother church. Built between 1877-82 to a John Oldrid Scott design at a reported cost of £50,000 (PDV £4.25 million), it was made a cathedral in 1922 with its diocese spanning all of Western Europe. A museum is housed in the basement. Surprisingly, the first church for this denomination was built in Soho, London as early as 1677.

99. London (Wood Green) (Cathedral status 1985-present; built 1871 & 1980-85). A former Methodist church, designed by the Reverend J.N. Johnson and built in 1871, it became a Greek Orthodox cathedral in 1985 following a five year restoration scheme.

67. Middlesbrough (Diocese established 1878-present; built 1985-87). The original Roman Catholic cathedral was built in 1876-8 by George Goldie shortly before the diocese was established in 1878. It fell into disrepair before finally being destroyed by fire in 2000. Its replacement on a new site was designed by Frank Swainston and Peter Fenton and was erected between 1985-7.

56. Newcastle-upon-Tyne (Diocese established 1850-present; built 1842-72 & 1901/2). The Roman Catholic parish church built between 1842-4 to a design by

Augustus W. N. Pugin became a cathedral in 1850. The 74 metre high tower dates from 1870-2 is by A.M. Dunn and E.J. Hansom whilst the 1901/2 baptistery was later altered to create a porch.

57. Northampton (Diocese established 1850-present; built 1844-64 & 1955-9). The earliest part of the current church of St Mary and St Thomas was a modest chapel dating from 1844 by Augustus W.N. Pugin which became a Roman Catholic cathedral in 1852. His son E.W. Pugin enlarged this structure in 1863/4 and reversed the orientation placing the altar in its west end. This was later changed back to its traditional east location in A.S. Herbert's 1955-9 rebuild which also saw the original chapel demolished.

95. Norwich (Diocese established 1976-present; built 1882-1910). Built as a parish church between 1882-1910 to the designs of George Gilbert Scott Jnr and his brother J.O. Scott, it was financed by the 15th Duke of Norfolk (see Arundel). It was raised to Roman Catholic cathedral status in 1976 for the newly established diocese of East Anglia. It was believed the original intention was to make St Pancras church in Ipswich (built 1860/1 by George Goldie) the cathedral for the diocese.

58. Nottingham (Diocese established 1850-present; built 1841-4). In 1841-4, Augustus W.N. Pugin designed this church which cost a reputed £15,000 (PDV £1.47 million) before it became a Roman Catholic cathedral in 1852.

59. Plymouth (Diocese established 1850-present; built 1856-67). The earlier church of St. Mary, completed in 1807 and since demolished, proved inadequate when it was made a Roman Catholic cathedral in 1850. A new one was built from 1856-8 on a different site, designed by Joseph A. and Charles F. Hansom, with its 68 metre spire added in 1866/7.

70. Portsmouth (Diocese established 1882-present; built 1880-1906). An earlier Roman Catholic church dating from 1792 was replaced between 1880-1906 to designs by John Crawley and Joseph S. Hansom. It became a cathedral in 1882.

60. Salford (Diocese established 1850-present; built 1844-8). The Roman Catholic church was built 1844-8 to a design by Matthew E. Hadfield, becoming a cathedral in 1852 for the diocese of Greater Manchester.

98. Sheffield (Diocese established 1980-present; built 1846-50). This Roman Catholic church was built 1846-50 by architect Matthew E. Hadfield becoming a cathedral in 1980 for the diocese of Hallam.

61. Shrewsbury (Diocese established 1850-present; built 1852-6). Following the establishment of a diocese in 1850, a Roman Catholic cathedral was built between 1852-6 to a design by Augustus W.N. Pugin, who unfortunately died prior to it commencing on site. The project was taken over and completed by his 18 year old son Edwin W. Pugin and cost a reported £4,000 (PDV £378,000).

103. Stevenage (Cathedral status 2002-present; built 2001/2). The Coptic Orthodox Church of Egypt in Stevenage is the sects first purpose-built church in this country and was opened in 2002 as a cathedral.

Appendix C - Further Reading and Notes in the Text

If you want to find out more about the various topics covered in this book, I would recommend the following titles which I have consulted during my research for this book:

Andrews, Francis B: *The Mediæval Builder and his Methods* (Barnes & Noble) 1925 reprinted 1993 – covers its subject from the 13th to 15th centuries in England and Europe.

Butler, Lionel and Given-Wilson, Chris: *Medieval Monasteries of Great Britain* (Michael Joseph) 1979 – a description of all the main monastic sites still surviving in this country including a useful background on the main monastic orders.

Cannon, Jon: *The Great English Cathedrals and the World that made them 600-1540* (Constable) 2007 – every twenty years or so a major new work appears on England's cathedrals. This is the most recent one with plenty of interesting information, graphics and illustrations.

Cobb, Gerald: *English Cathedrals: The Forgotten Centuries* (Thames and Hudson) 1980 - this book deals with ten cathedrals showing how they have changed from 1530 to the present day. Contains many illustrations to enhance the text.

Coleman, Terry: *The Railway Navvies* (BCA) 1972 - a book about the men who built the railways which has a lot of relevance to the cathedral constructors.

Cook, G.H: *The English Cathedral Through The Centuries* (Phoenix) 1957 - this book accomplishes its aim in providing the most authoritative single-volume work on the subject. Comprehensive and highly recommended.

Edwards, David L: *The Cathedrals of Britain* (Pitkins Pictorials) 1989 – well illustrated with some interesting text and background history on 18 cathedrals.

Erlande-Brandenburg, Alaine: *The Cathedral Builders of the Middle Ages* (Thames & Hudson) 1995 - this book deals with the cathedral builders of France, Germany, Italy and Spain as well as England with some good colour illustrations from contemporary manuscripts.

Fletcher, Sir Banister: *A History of Architecture* (The University of London) 18th edition 1975 - a scholarly and comprehensive global history of architecture with many wonderful sketches and detailed plans of English cathedrals and their continental cousins.

Harvey, John: *Cathedrals of England and Wales* (Batsford) 1974 - descriptions and plans of England and Wales medieval cathedrals including their building and significant designers. John Harvey has done more than anyone to discover and name the architects responsible for this country's cathedrals. Highly recommended.

Harvey, John: *The Mediæval Architect* (Wayland) 1972 – a book that demystifies the role of the architect in the medieval period including his education and methods.

Hewett, C.A.: *English Cathedral Carpentry* (Wayland) 1974 – a detailed account with magnificent line drawings of the functional carpentry found in England's medieval cathedrals.

Hislop, Malcom: *How To Build A Cathedral* (Bloomsbury) 2012 - lots of useful information with good sketches and illustrations.

Jeffery, Paul: *England's Other Cathedrals* (The History Press) 2012 - a useful history of England's lesser known, former cathedrals. Fascinating information on Henry VIII's proposed cathedrals, most of which were never created. Highly recommended.

Knoop, D and Jones G.P.: *The Mediæval Mason* (Manchester UP) 1967 – an economic history of English stone building in the late Middle Ages with some interesting insights into the conditions in which stonemasons lived and worked.

Kraus, Henry: *Gold was the Mortar – The Economics of Cathedral Building* (Routledge & Kegan Paul) 1979 – an interesting study of the financing problems encountered in building the medieval cathedrals of France, Germany and England with particular reference to York Minster.

Lehmberg, Stanford: *English Cathedrals – A History* (London) 2005 - particularly strong on the post-Reformation history of this country's cathedrals.

Maude, Thomas: *Guided by a Stone-Mason* (TPP) 2010 - a look at English churches through the eyes of a practising stone-mason using plain English.

Morris, Richard: *Cathedrals and Abbeys of England and Wales* (Dent) 1979 - an excellent account of 75 great churches covering the period from the 7th Century until the Reformation. Covers the history, the people involved, technology and function with contributions from archaeologists, engineers, art historians and liturgists. Highly recommended.

New, Anthony: *A Guide to the Cathedrals of Britain* (Constable) 1980 - detailed descriptions of British cathedrals of all faiths including some former ones.

Pevsner, Nikolaus Pevsner and Metcalf, Priscilla: *The Cathedrals of England* in two volumes (Penguin) 1985 – a comprehensive work covering England's Anglican and Roman Catholic cathedrals written by the prodigious 20th Century art and architectural chronicler.

Prior, Edward S: The Cathedral Builders in England 1905 (reprinted by Hard Press Publishing, USA) – some interesting observations in a book written in the early 20th Century.

Salzman, L.F.: *Building in England Down to 1540* (Oxford Clarendon Press) 1992 – a comprehensive and fascinating account of the building industry in the Middle Ages. Highly recommended.

Stenton, Sir Frank: *Anglo-Saxon England* (The Oxford History of England) 1967 – the second part of a scholarly and comprehensive series covering the history of England, this one deals with the period from the departure of the Romans up to and including the Norman Conquest.

Tatton-Brown, Tim: *Great Cathedrals of Britain* (BBC Books) 1989 – an excellent history of cathedrals and their dioceses written from an archaeology point of view.

Taylor, Richard: *How To Read A Church* (Rider) 2003 – a book that provides a useful background to Christianity, leading figures and church symbols which will be of particular interest to those with little knowledge of Christianity.

Notes on Numbers in the Text

1 - The Bishop of Lincoln possessed 40 manors, ten palaces and a castle in three other counties outside Lincolnshire in addition to a substantial London home.

2 - There has been much written about priest Elias of Dereham and monk Alan Walsingham involvement in the building of Ely's octagon and Salisbury Cathedral. They were obviously highly informed patrons but there is no hard evidence that they had any design or building technology skills to be considered as the architects of these two projects. See John Harvey: The Mediæval Architect page 82.

3 - Of the 20,000 in c1220, some 4,000 belonged to the Benedictine Order, 3,000 each to the Cistercians and Augustinians while 7,000 were nuns.

4 - The cathedrals of Durham, Norwich, Ripon, Wells, Winchester and York offered the right of sanctuary from persecution provided the fugitive remained within an area defined by a series of stones.

5 - For a full appraisal of this subject refer to Henry Klaus: *Gold was the Mortar* pages 133-153.

6 - The need to accommodate all the local populace for Christian worship appears more important for secular cathedrals than monastic ones. Out of England's 10 largest medieval cathedrals (in terms of floor area) four were secular including the biggest three: Old St Paul's, York, Lincoln and Salisbury (5th). Winchester (4th), Ely (6th), Durham (7th), Canterbury (8th), St. Albans (9th) and Norwich (10th) were cathedral priories. Incidentally Liverpool Anglican would be first and the current St Paul's would be third if post-Reformation cathedrals were to be also included.

7 - From John Harvey: *The Mediæval Architect* page 81.

8 - Of these 18, two were secular priests, three were Augustinian canons, five were monks, one was a Knights Templar, one a member of the house of St Robert of Knaresborough and six were lay-brothers (three Benedictine and three Cistercians). Only five were certainly both master masons and members of a religious order (one mason and two carpenters were the three Cistercians; Arnold a lay-brother at Crowland; Austin Canon Edmund of St Andrew was a master carver and carpenter). See John Harvey: *The Mediæval Architect* page 81.

9 - From L.F. Salzman: *Building in England Down to 1540* page 390.

10 - From John Harvey: *English Medieval Architects: A Biographical Dictionary down to 1550.*

11 - From L.F. Salzman: *Building in England Down to 1540* pages 4-5.

12 - From John Harvey: *The Mediæval Architect* page 103.

13 - From John Harvey: *The Mediæval Architect* page 78.

14 - From John Harvey: *The Mediæval Architect* pages 133-4.

15 - John Harvey: *Henry Yevele (sic), c1320-1400: The Life of an English Architect* (1946).

16 - In Shakespeare's play 'The Second Part of King Henry the Fourth Act 1 Scene 3', this process is described as "When we mean to build, We first survey the plot, Then draw the mould; And when we see the figure of the house, Then must we rate the cost of the erection." From L.F. Salzman: *Building in England Down to 1540* page 15.

17 - From L.F. Salzman: *Building in England Down to 1540* pages 380-1.

18 - From L.F. Salzman: *Building in England Down to 1540* pages 369-376.

19 - From L.F. Salzman: *Building in England Down to 1540* page 29.

20 - From L. Butler and C. Given-Wilson: *Medieval Monasteries of Great Britain.*

21 - From D. Knowles *The Religious Orders of England* Vol 3 pages 108-120.

22 - For a full analysis of these proposals I would refer the reader to Paul Jeffery: *England's Other Cathedrals* pages 66-94.

23 - A full description of this can be found in Stanford Lehmberg: *English Cathedrals – A History* pages 155-7.

24 - From Stanford Lehmberg: *English Cathedrals – A History* page 271.

Lightning Source UK Ltd.
Milton Keynes UK
UKOW06f2327110915

258476UK00001B/22/P